THE PRIDE

COLLECTED EDITION

THE PRIDE VOL. 1: I NEED A HERO Contains material originally published in magazine form as THE PRIDE #1-6 and THE PRIDE ADVENTURES #1-4 and the CARDIFF INDEPENDENT COMIC EXPO ANTHOLOGY. First printing 2016. Self-published by Joe Glass under the banner of Queer Comix.
© 2011 Joseph Glass and Gavin Mitchell. The Pride, its logo, all prominent characters featured therein and all other character likenesses therein are trademarks of Joseph Glass and Gavin Mitchell, unless otherwise noted. Queer Comix logo is trademark of Joseph Glass and Mike Stock. All rights reserved. No part of this publication may be reproduced or transmitted in any form or by any means (except for review purposes) without the express written permission of the authors. All names, characters, events & locales in this publication are entirely fictional. Any resemblance to actual persons (living or deceased), events without satiric intent, is coincidental unless otherwise stated. Printed in the UK by UK Comics. 1st Printing. The Pride and The Pride Adventures logos designed by Jason Gann. Wraparound cover by Ricardo Bessa

Facebook.com/ThePrideComic   @ThePrideComic   ThePride.bigcartel.com

C O N T E N T S

FOREWORD

Being a superhero is hard... Being a gay superhero is harder. In a world that's overrun with people of special abilities and things that are "different" what does it mean to actually be "different?" The Pride is a team of individuals who unlike their-at least seemingly-hetero counterparts, accept everyone they come in contact with... unless of course that person is a megalomaniacal Reverend with designs on world domination. Though honestly, with a little rehabilitation I'm sure he could sit with us too. *The Pride* is one of those books that parallels real-life struggles with the weighty decisions anyone in spandex has to make: to kill or not to kill, that is the question. It's about deciding what kind of hero you want to be. It's about accepting how you were born and convincing the world to accept you too.

Often times we take for granted the struggles of others. I'll admit, I've had a relatively easy time being as gay as I am. *The Pride* reminded me of a more entertaining *Queer as Folk* in that yeah the drama is heightened and personal struggles are punctuated with explosions but they still parallel people in our own world. It reminded me to check my vodka soaked drag-queen induced privilege and keep mindful that everyone's path is different. There are those out there who may seem "better off" but it took quite a fight to get there. *The Pride* isn't about the obvious insinuation of proudness or the connotation of a parade with free condom and lube samples, but more about coming together and accepting your common man, woman, non-binary person, and radioactive sewer mutant with an understanding that we all have a fight to win. Whether that's just to have our pronouns recognized, to overcome stereotypes, or just live on the surface with the rest of society...

Like everyone, each of the characters has their own personal struggle with acceptance, but they manage to find that common thread that bonds them together: peace. There's something we could all learn from the adventures of The Pride, it's that no matter who or what you are, you can always find your pride.

-Dax!

RUNNING ORDER

HOLDING OUT FOR A HERO

Written by Joe Glass, Art by Gavin Mitchell, Colors by Kris Carter, Letters by Mike Stock

FIREWORKS

Written by Joe Glass, Art by Gavin Mitchell, Colors by Kris Carter, Letters by Mike Stock

DON'T RAIN ON MY PARADE

Written by Joe Glass, Art by Dan Harris, Colors by Kris Carter, Letters by Mike Stock

YOU THINK YOU'RE A MAN

Written by Joe Glass, Art by Gavin Mitchell, Colors by Kris Carter, Letters by Mike Stock

CABARET

Written by Joe Glass, Art by Kendall Goode (pages 105-112), JD Faith (pages 113-115), Gavin Mitchell (pages 116-117), Jack Davies (pages 118-119), Chris Wildgoose (pages 120-123) & Marc Ellerby (pages 124-126), colors by Ben Wilsonham (pages 105-115 & pages 124-126), Letters by Mike Stock

FINALLY

Written by Joe Glass, Pencils by Maxime Garbarini, Inks and Colors by Héctor Barros, Letters by Mike Stock

The Pride Issue 1 - Cover by Kris Anka

"THIS MORNING, THE WORLD WAS SAVED FROM *CERTAIN* DESTRUCTION *ONCE AGAIN*, THANKS TO THE EFFORTS OF THE ENDLESSLY AWESOME, SUPERBLY WICKED *SUPERDUDE*."

"MEANWHILE, ON THE MOON, CRABMAN AND LOBSTERBOY FOILED A PLOT BY *ANGRY MOON-PEOPLE* TO DESTROY THE *WHOLE* WORLD."

"IT IS BELIEVED THE INSURGENT ALIENS WERE DEFEATED WITH A *NUCLEAR* TROUT."

BOOOM

KA-BOOM

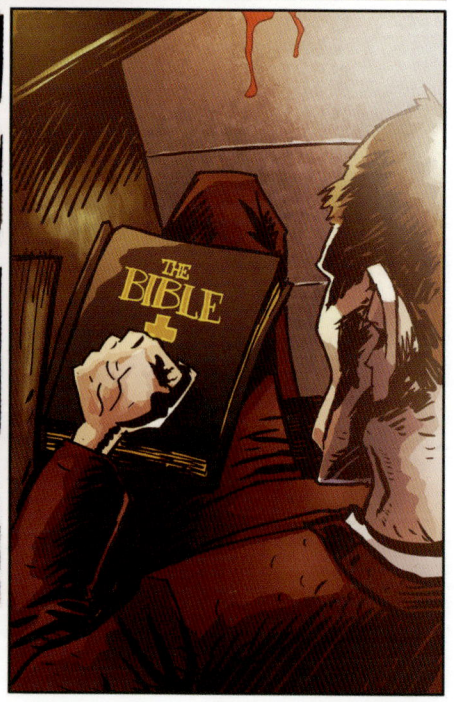

14

GROAN

NOW, NOW, DEAR. DON'T MOAN.

IF ONE DOES NOT WISH TO BE TAUGHT A LESSON IN HOW TO TREAT A LADY...

...ONE SHOULD NOT APPROACH *THE MASTER*.

HONEY, I FIGURE THESE GUYS HAVE LEARNED THEIR LESSON WELL.

AH, IF IT ISN'T OUR *FABULOUS* YANKEE DARLING. WHAT BRINGS YOU TO THIS *DELIGHTFUL* LITTLE CORNER OF THE WORLD?

I'VE A PROPOSITION TO MAKE, FROST.

DARLING, I HAD *NO IDEA* YOU SWUNG BOTH WAYS.

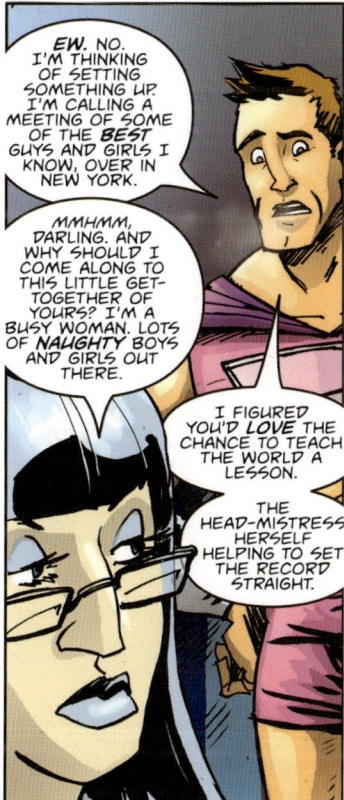

EW. NO. I'M THINKING OF SETTING SOMETHING UP. I'M CALLING A MEETING OF SOME OF THE *BEST* GUYS AND GIRLS I KNOW, OVER IN NEW YORK.

MMHMM, DARLING. AND WHY SHOULD I COME ALONG TO THIS LITTLE GET-TOGETHER OF YOURS? I'M A *BUSY* WOMAN. LOTS OF *NAUGHTY* BOYS AND GIRLS OUT THERE.

I FIGURED YOU'D *LOVE* THE CHANCE TO TEACH THE WORLD A LESSON.

THE HEAD-MISTRESS HERSELF HELPING TO SET THE RECORD STRAIGHT.

WELL, IT *HAS* BEEN A WHILE SINCE I GRACED THE COLONIES WITH MY PRESENCE. THE *USUAL PLACE*, I TAKE IT?

SURE, WHY CHANGE WHAT WORKS.

OF COURSE. WELL, IT *IS* AN INTERESTING PROPOSITION. DO SEE THAT YOU DON'T BORE ME.

los angeles

WHAT UP AMIGOS! HOW 'BOUT YA DROP TH' ROCK, AND LET *UNCL'* TYRONE MAKE YOUS A DEAL, EH?

UMM?

WE JUST PLAYIN' BALL, DUDE. WE DON'T WANT NO TROUBLE.

AIN'T *NO* TROUBLE YOU CAN BRING I AIN'T READY FOR, JUNIOR...

Y'SURE 'BOUT THAT, TY?

WHITE TRASH... *CHICA*, WHAT YOU DOIN' HERE? I AIN'T *PLAYIN'* NO GAME.

NAH, CUZ. BUT THESE KIDS *WERE*. THEY DON'T NEED ANY OF YOUR TROUBLE. *OR* ANY OF WHAT YOU'RE SELLING.

SORRY, *'CUZ'*, BUT NO ONE STEPS ON TYRONE, 'SPECIALLY NO FAGGOTY, @$$-LOVIN' SONOVA--

BLAM BLAM BLAM

BAD MOVE, TY.

FIVE MINUTES LATER...

THANKS, WT!

DON'T MENTION IT. JUST DO ME A FAVOUR...

... *DON'T* GET MIXED UP WITH TY'S CROWD. 'THE LIFE' AIN'T *NO* LIFE AT ALL.

SURE THING, WT!

AND HEY, WE KNEW YOU AIN'T *NO FAG*. YOU *KICKED ASS!*

I'D HAVE HELPED, BUT YOU SEEMED TO HAVE IT UNDER CONTROL. BUT THAT ASSUMPTION THEY HAD ABOUT US 'FAGS'... IT RUINS THE GOOD FEELING EVERY TIME, HUH?

FABMAN. PLEASURE TO MEET YOU.

I KNOW WHO YOU ARE. PLEASURE'S ALL MINE, MAN.

BUT THEY WERE JUST KIDS, DUDE. ATTITUDES CHANGE.

NOT QUICK ENOUGH THOUGH, RIGHT?

I'M LOOKING TO DO SOMETHIN' ABOUT THAT. YOU WANT IN?

...SURE.

NEW YORK CITY

HEY, FRUITIE! WHATCHA RUNNIN' FO'?

OOOF!

CRASH

HEY, I THOUGHT YOU QUEERS WAS MEANT TO BE GRACEFUL.

HEH, MEBBE HE'S JUST TOO EXCITED TO SEE US.

BIG BURLY MEN LIKE US. SISSY-BOY MUST BE TURNED ON.

P-PLEASE, J-JUST LEAVE ME ALONE, I'M NOT DOING ANYONE ANY HARM.

THAT'S WHERE WE FEEL DIFFERENTLY, SICKO. AIN'T NO PLACE FOR YOU HERE, OR ANYWHERE.

YEAH. THIS IS JUST A PUBLIC SERVICE 'BOUT TO HAPPEN HERE.

19

FINE, FINE. *THE S.L.G.B.T.* WE'RE GETTING OFF TRACK. THE REASON I CALLED YOU ALL HERE...

WELL, AREN'T YOU *FED UP* OF BEING MIS-REPRESENTED OUT THERE?

OF BEING A LAUGHING STOCK BECAUSE YOU OPENLY DISPLAY YOUR LIFESTYLE *AS WELL AS* YOUR SUPER-POWERS?

OR SICK THAT THE ONLY GAY PEOPLE YOU SEE ON TV ARE THESE *DESEXUALISED*, NON-THREATENING *JOKE MACHINES.*

HELL, THERE'S THE *AWESOME HERO ARRANGEMENT* (AHA!), THE *WONDROUS WARRIORS*, THE *TRULY GREAT SIX*, THE *FAMOUS FIFTY*, EVEN THE SUPER HEROIC ORGANISATION OF *EAST CORNWALL!*

BUT WHERE IS THE *GAY SUPER GROUP?* WHERE ARE THE *TRANSGENDER HEROES?*

WELL, YOU KNOW WHAT? THEY AIN'T OUT THERE. SO, THAT'S WHY I PROPOSE WE START *OUR OWN!*

HOW 'BOUT IT? WILL YOU ALL JOIN *THE PRIDE?*

UMMM, EXCUSE ME?

I'M HERE FOR THE S.L.G.B. MEETING--

S.L.G.B.T.!!

SHHH!

AND YOU ARE?

UMMM, MY NAME IS OWEN MERCURY. I, UMMM, DON'T HAVE A SUPER NAME. YET.

I JUST... I KEPT MY EAR TO THE GROUND. HEARD THIS MAY BE GOING ON, AND... WELL, I'D LIKE TO JOIN.

I CAME ALL THE WAY UP FROM SAN FRAN. I'M GAY. I WANT IN.

WELL, OKAY THEN OWEN. WHAT IS IT YOU CAN DO?

OH! HOLD ON...

HE DOES KNOW THIS *ISN'T* AN AUDITION FOR PORNOGRAPHY, YES?

QUIET, GIRL! LET THE BOY DO HIS THING.

UH, HONEY, WHAT ARE YOU DOING?

OH. UMM, THE SHIRT IS NEW, AND I LIKE THESE JEANS. I DIDN'T WANT TO RUIN THEM.

OOOHHHH -KAY...

WHAT DO YOU THINK?

I THINK WE GOT A TEAM, HONEY.

NOT YET. THERE'S JUST ONE MORE THING WE NEED...

SLAM!

LONG TIME NO SEE, WOLF.

FABS. WELCOME TO THE PARTY. PULL UP A STOOL.

OOOH, YOU KNOW HOW I *LOVE* PARTIES. WHERE'S THE GO-GO BOY?

AT TOYBOI. NOT EXACTLY ONE OF THOSE BARS, DUDE, SO TONE IT DOWN A NOTCH, WOULD'YA.

≳SIGH≲ FINE. YOU *KNOW* HOW MUCH I HATE HIDING MY FABULOUSNESS, DARLING.

IT'S EASY FOR YOU, WHAT WITH ALL YOUR PRACTICE IN THE CLOS--

DID YOU JUST CALL ME 'DUDE'?

THINGS CHANGE, QUEENY. THERE, HAVE A DRINK.

≳HACK≲ ≳COUGH≲ -HUR- ≳ECH≲!

BUT THEN SOME THINGS NEVER CHANGE.

25

HI, OH, HI. OOH, DON'T YOU LOOK THE *BAD* BOY!

YES. UMM, I'D LIKE A COSMO, PLEASE.

YOU KNOW WHAT? WHISKEY IS FINE.

WHAT DO YOU WANT?

THAT'S NICE.

FINE. I HAVE A PROPOSITION FOR YOU.

HOW MANY TIMES DO I HAVE TO SAY 'NO'?

HAHAHA, YOU'RE SO FUNNY I FORGOT YOU WERE SAD.

I'M PUTTING TOGETHER A TEAM, DEAR. I WANT YOU IN IT.

DON'T DO TEAMS. DON'T HERO NO MORE.

FUNNY. A LOT OF THE CRIMINAL ELEMENT SEEMS TO BE GETTING CAUGHT AROUND HERE LATELY. *VIOLENTLY,* I MIGHT ADD.

YOU ALWAYS WERE A BAD BOY, DEAR.

27

WOLF! OH MY GOD, I'M -- I'M *SUCH* A BIG FAN OF YOUR WORK!

UMM, THANKS, KID. AND YOU ARE?

THAT'S TWINK. NEW RECRUIT. ISN'T HE THE SWEETEST?

ERM, YEAH. I JOINED THE PRIDE, I'M JUST HOPING TO DO SOME GOOD Y'KNOW.

I'M LOOKIN' FORWARD T--

ULP!

CHRIST, FABS, ARE YOU *NOT* BOTHERING TO TRAIN THEM?

TO BE HONEST, I TRAINED MYSELF. NOT AS RIGOROUS AS YOU, BUT I TRIED TO FOLLOW YOUR METHODS, I-

WE ONLY STARTED *YESTERDAY*, WOLFIE. I WAS HOPING YOU'D HELP WITH THAT.

HERE, KID. YA DID GOOD. NOTHING A LITTLE TRAINING WON'T IMPROVE.

SO YOU'RE IN?

The Pride Issue 2 - Cover by Cory Smith and Kris Carter

WELL, YOU SAID YOU WANTED TO SEE WHAT I CAN DO.

fireworks

JOE GLASS
WRITER

GAVIN MITCHELL
ART

KRIS CARTER
COLOURS

MIKE STOCK
LETTERS

DELIGHTFUL.

DA-AMN, BOY!

I LOVE THE COSTUME.

...BUT... YOU DON'T HAVE ANY POWERS!

VERY IMPRESSIVE FOR A MORTAL.

YEAH, YEAH, ALL VERY GOOD, BUT HERE'S HOW I THINK WE'LL WORK THIS TEAM.

I'LL BE TEAM LEADER IN TITLE, BUT WOLF HERE HAS PLAYED WITH THE BIG BOYS IN JUSTICE DIVISION, SO HE'LL BE FIELD LEADER.

I'M ALSO GONNA LEAVE TRAINING UP TO WOLF. HE'S VERY GOOD AT ALL THIS RUNNING, SWEATING AND EXCRUCIATING ROUTINES BUSINESS.

THIS SOUND GOOD TO EVERYONE?

MAN, IF HE GETS ME FIGHTING AS GOOD AS THAT...

I'LL DO ANYTHING THE MAN SAYS DAY AND NIGHT!

HERE, HERE.

GOOD. TRAINING IS GOING TO START TOMORROW.

WE'LL HAVE A LATE ONE TOMORROW, BUT I SUGGEST YOU GUYS GET A GOOD NIGHT SLEEP.

SEE YOU GUYS THEN!

THAT WAS AWESOME TO SEE, MR... ERM, WOLF, SIR

NAMES BRIAN, KID. AND THANKS.

ODD OF YOU TO GIVE UP THE LEADERSHIP ROLE LIKE THAT, STEVE.

PLEASE. I MAKE A GREAT FRONT MAN FOR THE MEDIA, BUT YOU HAVE THE EXPERIENCE AND THE TRAINING.

I WANT TO IMPROVE THE WORLD'S PERCEPTION OF US. THAT'S NOT GONNA HAPPEN WITH A POORLY TRAINED TEAM. AND YOU'RE REALLY GOOD AT THE GRUNT WORK ANYWAY, DARLING

WELL, THAT WAS ALMOST A COMPLIMENT, FABS.

I SAY IT WITH LOVE, BRIAN. TOODLES. YOU BOYS PLAY NICE, NOW.

HERE, KID.

TH-THANKS.

WHOOPS.

AND IT'S OWEN, OWEN M—

MERCURY, YEAH I KNOW. I CHECKED YOU OUT ON OUR WAY OVER HERE.

OH.

DON'T WORRY, OWEN. I DO IT TO EVERYONE. IT'S A DETECTIVE THING. I LIKE TO KNOW EVERYTHING THAT'S GOING ON IN A ROOM.

OH. RIGHT. I GUESS. AFTER ALL, I KNOW A LOT ABOUT YOU, YOU BEING IN JUSTICE DIVISION AN' ALL. I NEVER UNDERSTOOD WHY YOU LEFT THOUGH.

I DIDN'T 'LEAVE'. I WAS FIRED.

OH.

UMM, WHY? IF THAT'S OKAY TO ASK?

HN.

YEAH. IT'S ONLY FAIR, KID.

35

EVERYONE KNOWS HOW I GOT INTO THE JUSTICE DIVISION.

I MANAGED TO TAKE DOWN EVERY CRIME BOSS IN CHICAGO, WITH ENOUGH EVIDENCE TO PUT THEM AND THEIR GANGS BEHIND BARS FOR DECADES.

THE BIGGEST RICO CONVICTION IN HISTORY.

THIS CAUGHT THE ATTENTION OF THE BIG BOYS, AND I JOINED THE BIG LEAGUES. IT WAS A POPULAR CHOICE.

OF COURSE, AROUND THIS TIME I MET FABS. HE KNEW I WAS GAY.

AND, WELL, HE WAS THE ONLY GUY IN THE BUSINESS I COULD TALK TO ABOUT IT.

I HADN'T TOLD THE DIVISION I WAS GAY. I DIDN'T FEEL READY.

I WAS SCARED, I SUPPOSE. SCARED THAT I'D LOSE MY EDGE, THAT THE CRIMINALS WOULDN'T FEAR ME ANYMORE.

OF COURSE, FABS WAS OUT AND PROUD. AND ONCE THAT FIRST PAPARAZZI CAUGHT A SNAP OF US TOGETHER...

ALL OF THE PAPERS STARTED RUNNING WITH THE STORY. WILD SPECULATIONS ABOUT ME AND HIM. I TRIED TO IGNORE IT, BUT I KNEW SOMETHING BAD WOULD COME OF IT.

AND THEN IT DID.

THEY CALLED A MEETING. THEY DIDN'T SAY WHAT IT WAS FOR.

DUDE, AWESOME! TAKE A SEAT.

I'LL STAND THANKS. WHAT'S THIS ABOUT?

ME AND THE GUYS JUST HAVE SOME ,LIKE, CONCERNS DUDE, AND WE THINK, LIKE, MAYBE IT'D BE WISE IF YOU COULD STEP DOWN.

WHAT?!

LOOK, IF YOU'RE CONCERNED ABOUT ME AND FABS, WE'RE NOT REALLY DATING OR ANYTHING. THAT'S ALL WILD SPEC–

DUDE, DUDE, CHILL.

IT'S NOT ABOUT WHETHER YOU GUYS ARE REALLY AN ITEM.

I DON'T–

IT'S ABOUT WHETHER YOU'RE PERCEIVED TO BE.

IT'S THE IMAGE IT CREATES.

WOLF, MY FRIEND, IT IS AS SIMPLE MATTER AS THIS: WE NEVER ASKED IF YOU ARE IN FACT GAY, BUT PEOPLE BELIEVE YOU ARE. IF YOU AREN'T THEN PERHAPS WE CAN COME UP WITH ANOTHER SOLUTION.

ARE YOU GAY?

...YES.

THEN THERE'S THE ISSUE, DUDE. WE HAVE A FAMILY-FRIENDLY IMAGE WE HAVE TO PROTECT, OR PEOPLE WON'T THINK ABOUT US THE SAME WAY ANYMORE.

THEY WON'T FEEL SAFE.

I'M SORRY, MAN, BUT I'M SURE YOU UNDERSTAND.

IT'D JUST, LIKE, LOOK BETTER IF YOU LEAVE THAN WE FIRE YOU, Y'KNOW?

AND THAT WAS THAT. THE END OF MY CAREER WITH THE DIVISION. AND BEING OUTED ALL IN ONE.

OH MY GOD, THOSE GUYS ARE JERKS! THERE MUST BE SOMETHING WE CAN DO?

NAH, IN A WAY THEY WERE RIGHT. THEY PROBABLY WOULD HAVE STARTED GETTING DAMAGING PRESS FROM SOME CORNERS OF THE MEDIA.

WHICH IS WHY FABS' PLAN MAY BE A GOOD ONE AFTER ALL. IMPROVE HOW PEOPLE SEE US.

EVEN IF IT IS THE FIRST PLAN THAT HE'S EVER STUCK TO.

BESIDES, I GET THE FEELING THEY WEREN'T ALL TOTALLY FOR THE IDEA. VENUSIAN ACTUALLY LOOKED KIND O' ASHAMED.

YOU THINK HE'S GAY?

NO, NO. HIS SPECIES HAVE NO CONCEPT OF GENDER.

TO EVEN CALL HIM MALE IS WRONG. IT'S JUST A FORM HE CHOOSES SO PEOPLE WOULD UNDERSTAND HIM.

HUH...YOU'RE PRETTY GOOD AT READING PEOPLE THEN, HUH?

GOTTA BE, KID.

SO YOU AND FABMAN NEVER—

OH GOD, NO!

HE'S JUST A FRIEND. HA!

COOL.

COOL?

OH, WOW, LOOKIT THE TIME!

GOTTA GET UP EARLY, GET READY FOR PRACTICE TOMORROW, LONG DAY, WHOO BOY, WHERE DOES THE TIME GO, HUH! OMG, NIGHT!

ERR, NIGHT?

SO WHAT'S THE WORD, BOSS.

THE WORD IS GOOD, AND TH' NAME IS REVEREND, BASHER. YOU'D DO WELL TO 'MEMBER THAT.

BUT THESE RESULTS. THE SCIENTISTS WERE RIGHT... BEFORE THEY ALL DIED, ANYWAY. THE PROCESS AIN'T QUITE WORKIN' YET.

AH NEED SOMETHING MORE. ANOTHA ELEMENT TO TH' PROBLEM I AIN'T QUITE GOT YET.

TH' DAMN X-CEL VIRUS, THE SUPERHUMAN SICKNESS IN MANY OF THE SO-CALLED 'HEROES' OF THIS DECADENT, SINFUL WORLD; THE IMMUNOLOGY IS SO STRONG IT ACT'LLY FIGHTS AGAINST MAH COMMANDS.

AH NEED A SPECIAL KIND O' SUPER. AH AIN'T FOUND IT YET...

...BUT BELIEVE ME, AH'M GONNA KEEP LOOKIN'.

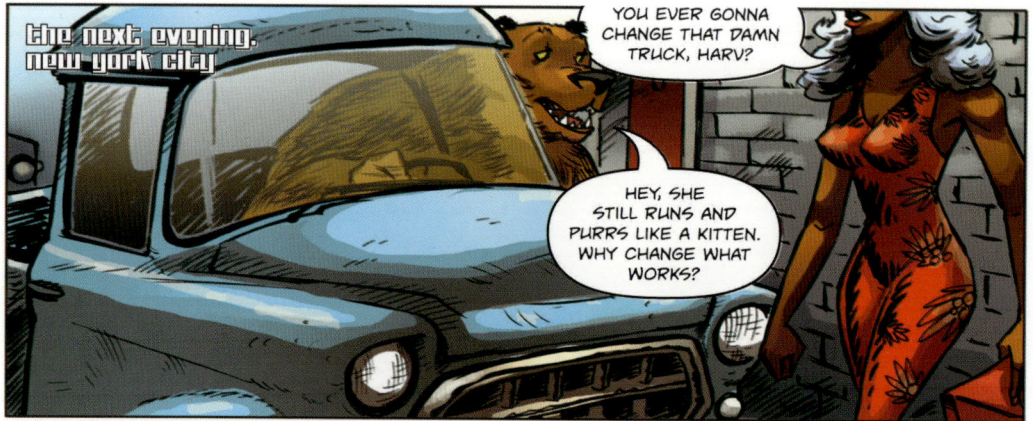

YOU EVER GONNA CHANGE THAT DAMN TRUCK, HARV?

HEY, SHE STILL RUNS AND PURRS LIKE A KITTEN. WHY CHANGE WHAT WORKS?

HONEY, THIS THING AIN'T NEVER WORKED.

I LIKE WHAT I KNOW, ANGEL.

WELL, THIS TEAM THING IS NEW TO US, DARLIN'. WHAT YOU MAKIN' OF IT?

I DUNNO. COULD WORK. COULD BE A MASSIVE DISASTER.

BUT HEY, FABS MEANS WELL, AND IT'S WORTH A SHOT.

YOU KNOW ME, ALWAYS TRYIN' TO MAKE A GOOD IMPRESSION.

FIERCE, HONEY. *FIERCE.*

Fantabulosa

YOU SURE YOU'RE UP TO THIS, HARVEY?

I'M FINE, ANGEL.

40

HEY, WHITE TRASH, RIGHT?

SURE. BUT PLEASE, MAN, MY NAME'S WAYNE.

I DIDN'T GET THE CHANCE TO SAY YESTERDAY, DUDE, BUT I'M A BIG FAN.

I REALLY RESPECT THE GOOD EXAMPLE YOU TRY TO SET, AND THE WAY YOU HELP OUR COMMUNITY.

NOT JUST BY FIGHTIN' CRIME, BUT WITH KNOWLEDGE AND SUPPORTING THE GOOD CAUSES.

TAKES A SPECIAL KINDA HERO TO DEVOTE THAT MUCH OF HIMSELF TO IT, MAN.

HEH, THANK YOU, WAYNE. THAT MEANS A LOT, BUDDY.

BUT HEY, MAYBE WITH THIS TEAM THING WE CAN ALL MAKE A DIFFERENCE.

OH PLEASE, BOYS, CAN YA KEEP THE FLIRTIN' TO YOURSELVES?

BUT ANGEL, DARLING, WE'D MISS OUT ON THE SCINTILLATING CONVERSATION.

UH HUH. AND WHY YOU TRAMPING IT UP BACK HERE, ICE MAMA.

FROST, DEAR. BUT IT'S AN EASY MISTAKE, I'M SURE.

NEW SECURITY MEASURES, DARLINGS. STAND UP STRAIGHT NOW.

GOOD POSTURE IS A GOOD START TO ALL THIS TRAINING NONSENSE, I'M SURE.

WHOOSH!

ANYONE ELSE GETTING' KINDA EXCITED?

DOWN BOY.

UH, WHAT'S WITH ALL THESE DUDES?

I BELIEVE THAT OUR FEARLESS AND STUNNINGLY IMPRESSIVE FIELD LEADER IS MAKING SOME CHANGES TO THE HQ HERE.

COME NOW, THE TRAINING ROOM AWAITS.

PROBABLY FOR THE BEST. WHOEVER HEARD OF A SUPERTEAM BASED IN A BAR?

OOF.

I FEAR THIS WILL BE DREADFULLY DROLE.

HONEY, I'M MORE WORRIED ABOUT BREAKING A NAIL. I MEAN, WHO KNOWS WHAT THAT BEAST WILL HAVE US DOING?

OH MY—

*@5K!

WHOOSH!

RRRRAAAAAHH!

CLANG!

ENOUGH!

YOU FOUGHT WELL, YOUNG WARRIOR.

YEAH, YOU DID GOOD, KID.

THANKS.

HOWEVER, THAT GUARD WASN'T PERFECT. THERE WERE AT LEAST FIFTEEN POSSIBLE TAKE-DOWN POSITIONS AVAILABLE TO THE QUEEN HERE, AT LEAST TWO OF WHICH WERE POTENTIALLY LETHAL.

YOU MAY BE ARMOURED UP, KID, BUT WE HAVE NO IDEA OF THE LIMITS OF THAT ARMOUR YET.

YOUR FIGHTING TECHNIQUE WAS OF COURSE FLAWLESS, YOUR MAJESTY.

PLEASE, YOU MAY CALL ME BY MY BIRTH NAME, SAPPHIRE, BRAVE WOLF.

THANK YOU. IT IS AN HONOUR.

IF I MAY SAY THEN, YOU DIDN'T SEEM TO GIVE MUCH REGARD TO MY POSITION BEHIND YOU. YOU'VE FOUGHT ALONE FOR SO LONG, YOU'VE BECOME USED TO IT. NOW YOU FIGHT WITH A TEAM AGAIN, YOU MAY WANT TO BE MORE AWARE OF THOSE THAT FIGHT WITH YOU.

AS FOR YOU GUYS, YOU WERE SUPPOSED TO BE HERE HOURS AGO.
I KNOW THAT FABS PICKED YOU ALL, BUT IF YOU'RE NOT TRAINED, I WILL RELEGATE YOU TO HQ POSITIONS AND KEEP YOU OFF THE FIELD.
MY, MY, WHAT A ROUGH HAND YOU HAVE.
YEAH, I'M AFRAID THAT'S JUST THE WAY I AM. WE'RE GOING TO BE THROWING OURSELVES INTO SOME REALLY DANGEROUS SITUATIONS.
AND WE NEED TO BE READY FOR THAT, SO YES, TRAINING WILL BE HARD, SOMETIMES BRUTAL.
SOME OF YOU HAVE FOUGHT ALONE FOR SOME TIME, BUT NOW WE NEED TO WORK TOGETHER AS A TEAM, NOT GET IN EACH OTHERS WAY, CAUSING AS MUCH PROBLEMS AS WHAT-EVER BAD GUY OF THE MONTH WE'RE UP AGAINST.
BUT AT THE END OF THIS TRAINING, WE'LL BE GREAT, MAYBE EVEN PERFECT. AND WE'LL BE ABLE TO HANDLE ANYTHING.
SO HOW ABOUT IT? YOU GUYS READY?
BOOOOOOM

moments later

WHAT?

MY METAL ARMOUR WOULD JUST HEAT UP IN THERE. I'D BE A DANGER TO ANYONE INSIDE.

HN. GOOD CALL.

HEAD AROUND BACK. IF THERE'S ANYONE TRYING TO GET OUT THAT WAY, YOU CAN HELP THEM.

ANGEL!

YOUR POWERS TO CREATE CONFUSION COULD BE A PROBLEM TOO. YOU STAY OUT HERE ON CROWD CONTROL.

I CAN'T GO IN.

SURE THING, HONEY!

YOU HEARD THE MAN, DARLINGS! NO ONE'S GETTING PAST THIS LINE.

WHAT LIN—?OOF?

THAT ONE, HONEY!

BEAR?

CAN'T GET ANY SCENTS. OVER THE SMOKE AND MY OWN BURNING FUR, ANYWAY.

I CAN'T SEE ANYTHING EITHER. WE NEED TO CLEAR SOME OF THESE FIRES!

FROST!

ALREADY DONE, DARLING. I'M GETTING THIS PLACE UNDER CONTROL.

CREAAAH

SISTER!

FROST, ARE YOU WELL?

I'M FINE, DEAR. MY, BUT YOU ARE A STRONG ONE.

AYE, AS ARE YOU TO SHOW NO FEAR IN THE FACE OF SUCH DISASTER. A WARRIOR BORN, PERHAPS?

SIMPLY BRITISH STIFF UPPER-LIP, MY DEAR.

WELL, THE FIRE'S DEAD HERE NOW. CAN YOU PICK UP ANYTHING?

THUDD

THAT WOULD BE ME, DEAR.

AS YOU MAY HAVE NOTICED IT'S GOT A BIT CHILLY IN HERE. TOO CHILLY FOR YOU'RE SILLY LITTLE FIREWORKS, I'M AFRAID.

PART ONE OF THIS LESSON IS NOW OVER, I BELIEVE IT'S TIME TO ADMINISTER PART TWO.

F@8$ THIS!

YOU GUYS TAKE CARE OF THE HOSTAGES, I'LL GET THIS IDIOT.

51

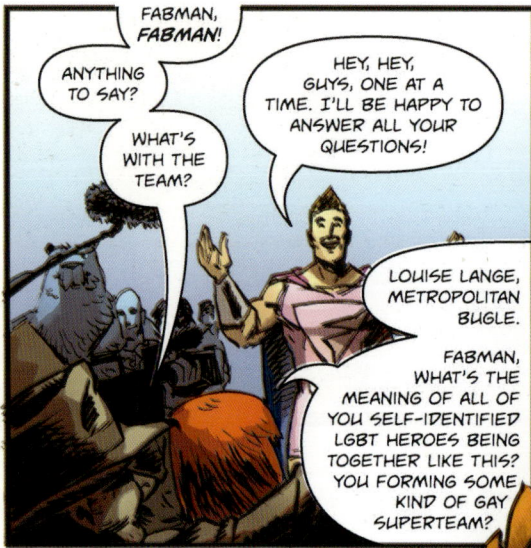

The Pride Issue 3 - Cover by Cory Smith and Kris Carter

WTN NEWS
THE PRIDE' CLAIM TO BE A NEW AND ORIGINAL SUPERHERO TEAM COMPRISED ENTIRELY OF GAY, LESBIAN, BISEXUAL AND TRANSGENDER MEMBERS.
ALTHOUGH SOME REPORTS INDICATE THERE HAVE BEEN OTHER SUCH TEAMS IN ENGLAND AND ELSEWHERE.
'THE PRIDE' MADE THEIR EXPLOSIVE DEBUT YESTERDAY WHEN THEY STOPPED AN ARSON ATTACK BY SUPER-CRIMINAL AND WHITE SUPREMACIST, FIREBOMB.
MOST OF THE MEMBERS OF THE TEAM ARE KNOWN 'SUPERHEROES' THAT HAVE BEEN ACTIVE INDEPENDENTLY UP TO THIS POINT. THEY CLAIM TO HAVE COME TOGETHER TO 'HELP EVERYONE' AND 'SHOW THE WORLD WHAT THE LGBT COMMUNITY CAN DO'.
BUT WHO EXACTLY ARE 'THE PRIDE'?
P STORY: GAY SUPERHERO TEAM OTHER NEWS: FIREB
GAY SUPERHERO TEAM: COMPRISING OF LGBT SUPERS, THE NEW TEAM PREVENTED THE DEATHS OF DOZENS AT THE HANDS OF THE ARSONIST, FIREBOMB. EVENTS TOOK PLACE AT A GAY BAR IN NEW YORK CITY.

--INDUSTRIES CEO BRIAN WILDE HAS ANNOUNCED THAT HE AND HIS COMPANY ARE FINANCIALLY BACKING AND EQUIPPING NEW GAY SUPERHERO TEAM, THE PRIDE.

HER NEW... 'ILDE INDUSTIES BACK PRIDE - LEAD

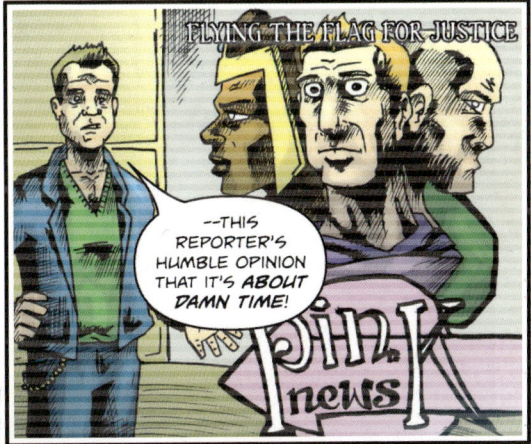

FLYING THE FLAG FOR JUSTICE

--THIS REPORTER'S HUMBLE OPINION THAT IT'S *ABOUT DAMN TIME!*

Pink news

I'M CALLING OUR LAWYERS NOW, BEAR.

HH.

CAT'S OUT OF THE BAG NOW, HUH, CUZ.

BIG WHO...

I DO NOT BELIEVE I LIKE THIS 'GRAHAM BUCK'.

DUNK!

I THINK IT'S ONLY FAIR TO HAVE A GAY SUPERHERO TEAM OUT THERE.

BUT WITH ALL THOSE OTHER SUPER TEAMS OUT THERE, NICK, ARE THEY NEEDED?

...AY ON OLIVE GAY SUPERHEROES: DO WE NEED THEM?

AND WHAT EXACTLY IS THEIR MISSION?

THEY'RE 'FOR EVERY-ONE'... AS LONG AS WE START GOING TO THEIR CLUBS?

VX NEWS

IS THIS AN EFFORT TO TAKE OVER AMERICAN CULTURE IN A GUERRILLA URBAN UNDERGROUND MOVEMENT?

ARE THEY REALLY SECRET ENFORCERS OF THE GAY AGENDA?

GRAHAM BUCK

59

I, UH, I'M JUST GOING TO GET SOME AIR.

OWEN? YOU OKAY, KID?

UH, SURE, I... I, UMMM, I---

YOU DIDN'T KNOW I WAS HIV POSITIVE.

NO, I--

TNK!

UH, SORRY. NERVES.

IT'S OKAY.

I GUESS, I JUST HAVEN'T EVER MET ANYONE WHO WAS POSITIVE BEFORE--

THAT YOU KNOW OF.

YEAH, AND WELL, I GUESS I DON'T KNOW MUCH ABOUT IT AND WELL, ISN'T IT...

ISN'T IT KIND OF DANGEROUS? I MEAN, GIVEN WHAT WE DO...

YOU MEAN, CAN YOU CATCH IT?

NO!

...YES...

I'M SO SORRY.

KID, YOU HAVE NOTHING TO APOLOGISE FOR. NO ONE EVER TALKS ABOUT THIS, AND FEW EDUCATE ABOUT IT. HELL, IT WAS NEVER MENTIONED TO ME GROWING UP.

TO ANSWER YOU'RE CONCERNS, NO, YOU CAN'T JUST CATCH IT.

AIN'T NOTHIN' WE'RE GONNA DO THAT PUTS YOU AT RISK. IT PASSES THROUGH BODILY FLUIDS, NOT BODY CONTACT. AND I'M HOPIN' YOU'RE NOT PLANNIN' ON A LOT OF THAT HAPPENING.

HEH, NO.

BUT, I MEAN, IS IT HEALTHY FOR YOU? AREN'T YOU, TECHNICALLY, LIKE, ILL?

TRUTH IS, KID, I TAKE GOOD CARE OF MYSELF. MY VIRAL COUNT IS LOW, I TAKE MY MEDS, AND I'M GETTING GOOD EXERCISE DOING THIS CRAZY THING WE DO.

HIV ISN'T THE DEATH SENTENCE IT ONCE WAS. THERE'RE TREATMENTS, AND WE CAN LIVE A NORMAL LIFE, IF WE TAKE GOOD CARE OF OURSELVES.

AND IF WE'RE SMART, AND KEEP SAFE, THEN THERE'S NOTHING TO WORRY ABOUT. YOU CAN'T JUST CATCH IT BY BEING NEAR ME. SO YOU OKAY NOW, KID?

YEAH...THANKS, YEAH, THAT HELPED. SORRY FOR GETTING ALL WIGGED OUT BY IT.

NOT AT ALL, KID. SADLY, IT HAPPENS ALL THE TIME.

HEY GUYS!

WE ARE GETTING, LIKE, LOADS OF CALLS FROM THE MEDIA RIGHT NOW, AND I COULD REALLY USE THE HELP.

ALL HANDS ON DECK!

SO, OKAY GUYS, MAYBE WE SHOULD CALL IT A DAY WITH THIS.

I THINK WE MAY NEED TO GET SOMEONE IN HERE FULL TIME TO DO THIS KINDA THING. I COULD USE SOME HELP WITH THAT WOLF.

SURE.

BUT DON'T WORRY, I WON'T BE ASKING YOU GUYS TO DO THIS AGAIN.

GOOD, BECAUSE THIS WAS A COLOSSAL WASTE OF OUR TIME.

IF WE'RE GOING TO BE A SUPERHERO TEAM OUT THERE IN THE THICK OF IT, WE'VE GOT TO TRAIN.

I UNDERSTAND WHAT YOU'RE TRYING TO DO, FABS, BUT ACTIONS SPEAK LOUDER THAN WORDS. WE SHOULD MAKE SURE OUR ACTIONS COUNT.

TWINK... YOU LOOK LIKE YOU'VE SEEN A GHOST.

OH. HA, NO NOT A GHOST. ON THE PHONE... IT WAS MY MOM AND DAD...

I'VE... I'VE NOT SPOKEN TO THEM IN A WHILE. NOT SINCE THEY SENT ME TO SOME CAMP; TO "CURE" ME OF MY POWERS.

IT'S A LONG STORY.

WELL, KID, YOU KNOW WHERE I AM. YOU NEED TO TALK, I'M HERE.

...THANKS. THAT MEANS A LOT.

63

training room

YOU HAVE TO TRAIN WITH THE TEAM!

HOOKER, I KNOW HOW MY POWERS WORK, OKAY? I DON'T NEED NO TRAINING; I'M AS BADASS AS I'LL EVER BE.

WHAT SHE SAID... BUT WITH BETTER VOCABULARY, NATURALLY.

GUYS...

C'MON ANGEL, IT'S ACTUALLY KINDA FUN. BEST EXERCISE I'VE HAD IN A WHILE.

BESIDES, IT CAN'T HURT. REMEMBER THE FIRST TIME WE TEAMED UP AND YOU MADE THOSE THUGS THINK I WAS AN ACTUAL BELOVED TEDDY BEAR?

AND WE STILL ARRESTED THOSE FOOLS.

YEAH, CRYIN' THEIR EYES OUT 'CAUSE BIG DADDY IN BLUE WAS TAKING THEIR CUDDLY BEAR FROM THEM.

INCIDENTALLY, WHAT EXACTLY ARE YOUR POWERS, ANGEL, DEAR?

TELEPATHY?

NOT EXACTLY.

I MAKE A FIELD OF CONFUSION. IT OBVIOUSLY WORKS ON A TELEPATHIC LEVEL, BUT I AIN'T CONTROLLING MINDS.

PEOPLE HALLUCINATE, MAYBE THINK THINGS ARE WHERE THEY AREN'T, THAT KINDA THING, HONEY.

SO I KNOW EXACTLY WHAT I'M DOING, HONEY. HELL, WHAT ABOUT THAT FIREBOMB FOOL YESTERDAY...

INDEED, DARLING. WE BEAT THAT MORON WITH A MINIMUM OF FUSS AND SWEAT.

AND WHAT IF THAT WAS A FLUKE?

EXACTLY WHAT WE WERE THINKING--

THE JUSTICE DIVISION!
OH LOOK, A FAN.
I MEAN, YOU GUYS SHOULDN'T EVEN, LIKE, BE OUT THERE IF YOU'RE NOT ALL TRAINED AND WHATEVER.

Manhole

manhattan, new york

HERE YA GO, MAN. SORRY ABOUT THE KNOCK EARLIER, DUDE.

NOT A PROBLEM, WAYNE, REALLY. BUT THANKS.

SO, THIS SEEMS LIKE A COOL PLACE. REMINDS OF THIS GREAT LITTLE PLACE IN CALI. IF YOU'RE EVER DOWN MINE, YOU SHOULD TOTALLY CHECK IT OUT.

THAT AN INVITATION?

I GUESS IT IS, YEAH.

WHERE YOU STAYIN' ANYHOW?

BEEN CRASHIN' AT A MOTEL.

Y'KNOW, YA COULD CRASH AT MINE. IT'S CHEAPER.

WELL, I WAS GETTING STRAPPED FOR CASH. SOUNDS GOOD.

fantabulosa

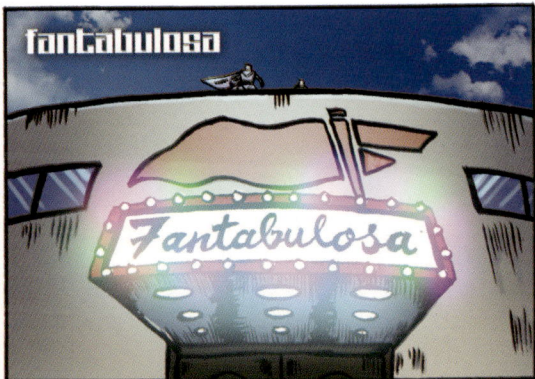

STEPHEN? ARE YOU OKAY?

YES. NO. ARE YOU?

I MEAN, THAT WHOLE DRAMA EARLIER... WHAT A MESS.

WERE THEY RIGHT? ARE WE DOING THE RIGHT THING? DID THIS WORLD REALLY NEED AN LGBT SUPERHERO TEAM?

WHY NOT? IT'S A DIVERSE WORLD, BUT SOMETIMES, WHEN WE LOOK AT THE HEROES OF THIS PLACE... CAN YOU SEE THAT?

LOOK AT THE JUSTICE DIVISION?

OUT OF A TEAM AS BIG AS THEY ARE, ONLY ONE MEMBER IS BLACK.

ONLY TWO ARE WOMEN, AND THEIR NEVER THE SPOKESPERSONS FOR THE TEAM. AND MORNINGSTAR TOO IS RARELY SEEN AS A FACE FOR THE TEAM.

THEY'RE SO WORRIED OF OFFENDING THE SENSIBILITIES OF A BIG, WHITE WORLD, THEY'RE TOO SCARED TO CELEBRATE THEIR DIFFERENCES.

THIS TEAM... AS WELL AS RIGHTING WRONGS AND FIGHTING FOR JUSTICE, WE CELEBRATE WHAT'S DIFFERENT.

WE CAN SHOW PEOPLE WE'RE UNAFRAID, AND THAT'S AN IMPORTANT MESSAGE TO GET OUT THERE. FOR EVERYONE.

YOU'RE RIGHT.

I JUST HOPE WE'RE READY.

77

TO BE CONTINUED...

The Pride Issue 4 - Cover by Jack Lawrence

UGH, IF THERE IS NO COFFEE HERE I MAY SIMPLY *DIE*, DARLING.

KOPI LUWAK, DARLIN'. ONLY THE BEST FOR US *FABULOUS* GIRLS.

YOU, YOU ARE A *GODSEND*, DARLING.

OKAY, I'LL BITE. HOW THE HELL DO YOU LOOK THIS GOOD AT *THREE* IN THE MORNING, ANGEL.

I MEAN, DID YOU GET UP IN DRAG *JUST* TO COME HERE?

CUZ, I WAS WORKIN' A SHOW OVER IN JULIO'S ON THE WEST SIDE. I *JUST* CAME FROM THE PLACE.

UMM, WHAT ARE WE ALL DOING HERE AT THREE IN THE MORNING ANYWAY?

I GOT THE CALL FROM BEAR, BUT HE'S NOT HERE...

I'LL TELL YA WHY...

SOMEONE'S GOT MY SON!
YOU THINK YOU'RE A MAN
WRITTEN BY JOE GLASS
ART BY HÉCTOR BARROS
COLOURS BY NATHAN ASHWORTH
LETTERS BY MIKE STOCK

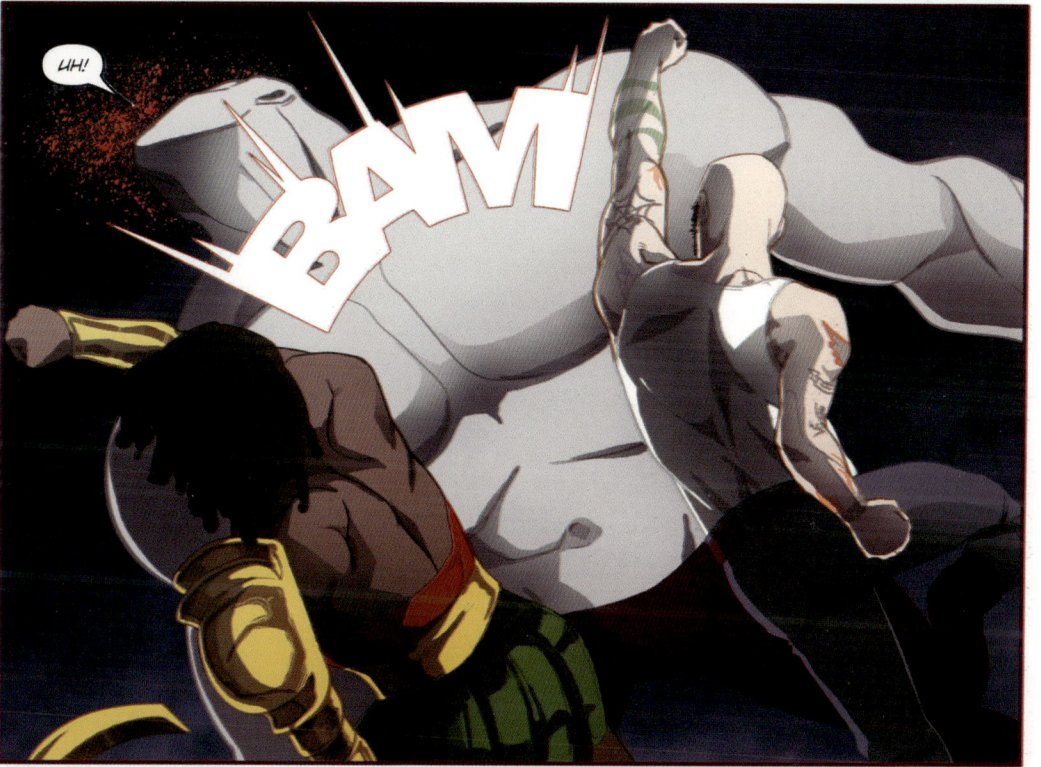

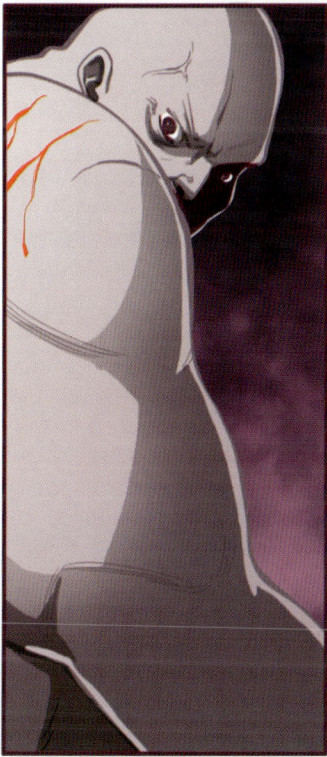

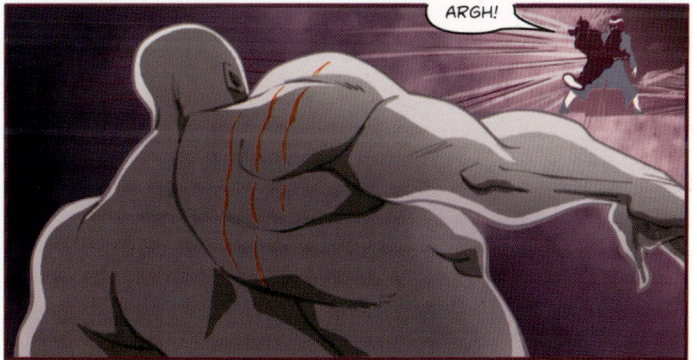

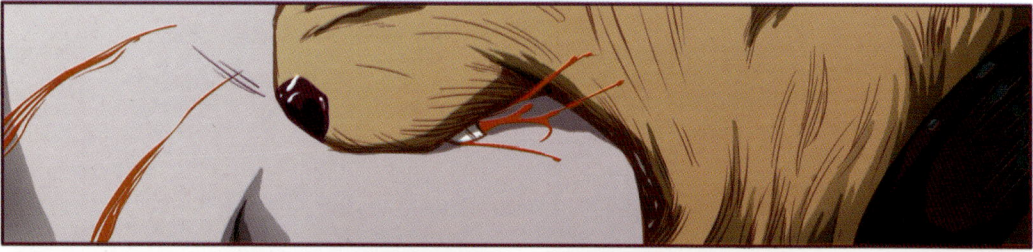

SMATBOOM!

FABS! QUICK! GET AFTER HIM, DAMMIT!

Thanks Maxime, Samir & JOE

TO BE CONTINUED...

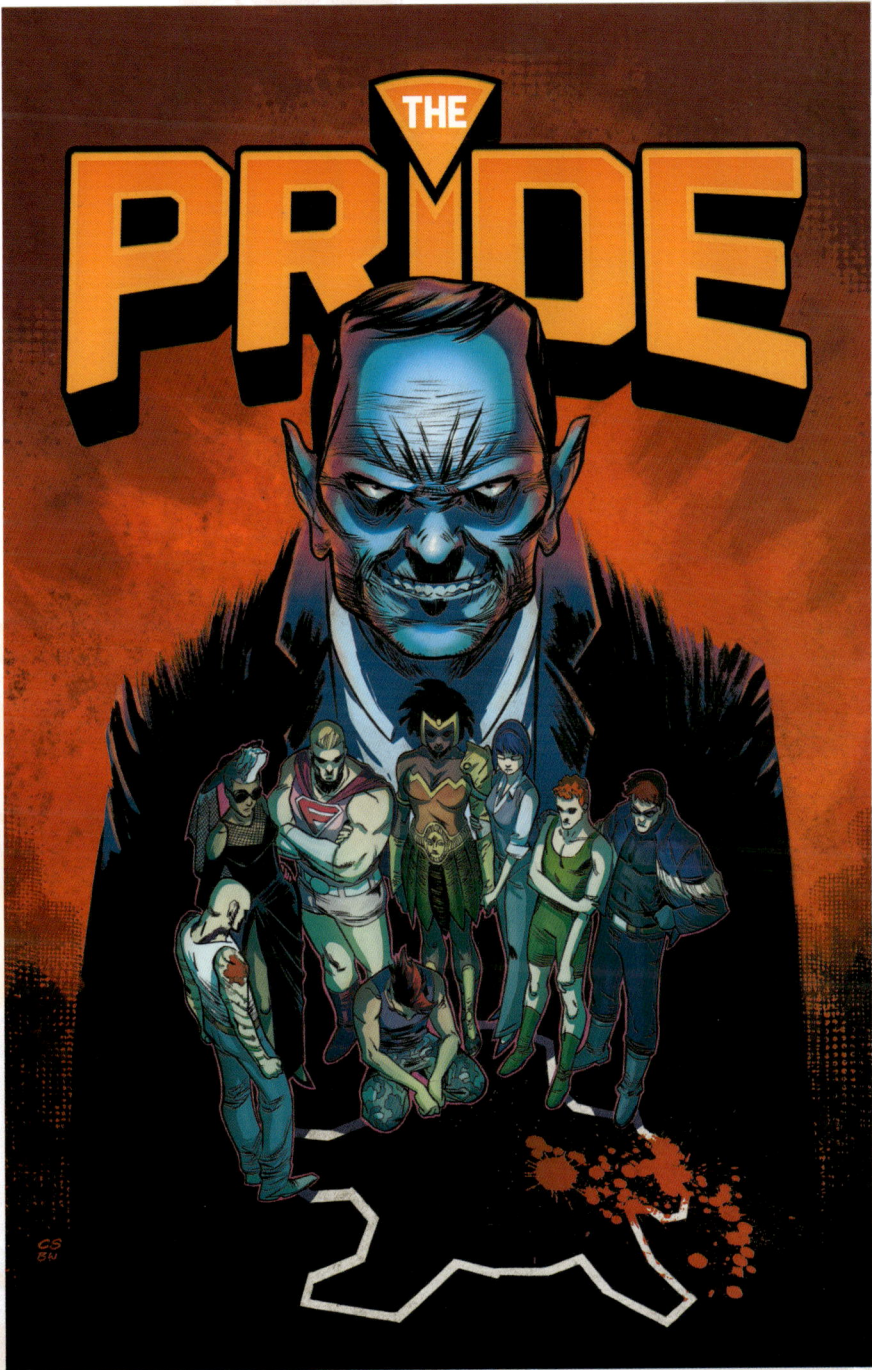

The Pride Issue 5 - Cover by Cory Smith and Ben Wilsonham

THE THINGS THEY'RE SAYIN'... *IT'S DISGUSTING!* WHAT KIND OF GOD—

THERE'S *NO GOD* IN WHAT THEY DO, KID. THEY'RE JUST A BUNCH OF HATEFUL, *SCARED* PEOPLE.

YEAH? HOW CAN YOU BE SO SURE? I OUGHTA *GUT* THE LOT OF 'EM.

HOW CAN WE HAVE A WAKE, WOLF?

WE DON'T EVEN HAVE A BODY. I MEAN, *MAYBE* HE'S NOT DEAD. *MAYBE* HE'LL COME BACK.

YOUR FATHER WAS A *GOOD MAN*, JAKE. HE'LL *ALWAYS* BE WITH US.

BASHER CAN *NEVER* TAKE THAT AWAY FROM YOU.

THANKS, TWINK.

DUDE, YOU CAN CALL ME OWEN.

BUT I'M STILL GONNA FIND BASHER.

AN' I'M GONNA MAKE HIM PAY.

KID, REVENGE IS *NEVER* THE WAY.

THAT BEING SAID, YOU CAN JOIN US, *AT LEAST* 'TIL WE FIND YOUR FATHER.

BUT... I'M *NOT* GAY, WOLF. I'M NOT LIKE MY DAD THAT WAY.

DOESN'T MATTER. THAT'S *NOT* WHAT WE'RE ABOUT.

TH- THANK YOU.

IT'S OKAY, KID. YOU GOT US.

HEY, IT'S OK, IT'S—

UH, *WHO'S THAT?*

109

JAKE. YOUR DAD... YOUR DAD WAS THE BEST FRIEND A MAN COULD EVER HAVE. HE WAS *AMAZING*.

THANK YOU.

SIR, IF YOU DON'T MIND US ASKING... HOW DID YOU KNOW HARVEY?

I'M KELE AMOS.

GUYS, IT'S ME... *ANGEL*.

MY *GOD*, ANG--*KELE*... IT'S A PLEASURE TO MAKE YOUR ACQUAINTANCE.

HOLY!

HEH. THANKS.

AND THIS IS MY WIFE, MICHELLE.

WELL, *DAMN*, KELE, YOU LUCKED OUT THERE, HUH.

MMHM, HE *SURE* DID, HONEY.

YOU'RE *STRAIGHT!?*

HA! ACTUALLY, I'M *PANSEXUAL*, OWEN. GENDER REALLY DOESN'T COME INTO IT FOR ME.

YOU'RE *BLOWIN'* MY MIND RIGHT NOW, DUDE.

WE'RE GONNA **GET** THE MUTHA WHO DID THIS TO HIM, JAKE. YOU CAN **BET YOUR ASS** WE WILL.

I HEAR YA.

⊰SIGH⊱ LOOK AT ME ⊰SNF⊱ STILL, **GREAT** TURN OUT FOR THE MAN.

THOUGH WHERE'RE FABS AND W.T.?

FABS HAS TAKEN IT **REALLY** HARD. WAYNE WENT LOOKING FOR HIM.

UH-HUH... WELL, I NOTICE **FROST** AIN'T HERE EITHER.

ALWAYS KNEW SHE WAS A **COLD** ASS B--

112

FROST. I HAVE FOUND YOU.

THAT YOU HAVE, DEAR.

COME NOW, TAKE A SEAT. THERE'S PLENTY OF BUBBLY FOR EVERYONE.

back at fantabulosa
the training room
I JUST WISH WE COULD DO MORE. IT'S BEEN WEEKS, AND WE STILL HAVE NO LEADS.
WE'LL GET THERE, TRUST ME.
BUT RIGHT NOW...
YOU SHOULD REALLY KEEP YOUR MIND IN THE GAME.
THERE'S NO WAY OUT OF THIS HOLD. I GOT YOU DEAD TO RIGHTS, KID.
UGH!
TNK
WHU-?
GRRRRA AAAAH!
TNK
THUN

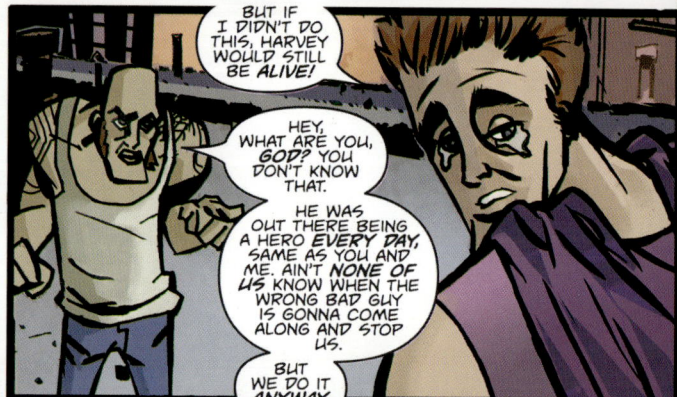

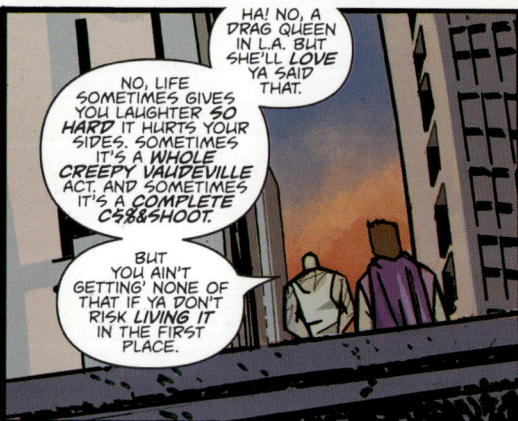

elsewhere

YOU SEEM HAPPY, BO—

REVEREND.

OH, SON, AH AM HAPPY! THE TIME OF REVELATION IS AT HAND!

TH' MACHINE IS READY! AND WITH IT, HUMANITY'S LOYALTY AND FAITHFULNESS TO GOD 'N' ME.

SO WHAT'S THIS THING DO, ANYHOW?

WHEN AH SWITCH IT ON, ALL O' TH' SO CALLED HEROES IN THE WORLD WILL HEAR MY VOICE. IT'LL BE SCREAMIN' IN THEIR VERY BLOOD.

I'LL TAKE CONTROL OF THE VIRUS THAT BIRTHED THESE MONSTROSITIES BEFORE TH' EYES OF TH' LORD, AN' AH'LL MAKE 'EM DO GOD'S WORK. MAH WORK.

AN' THOSE THAT DON'T LISTEN?

AH'LL BURN THEM DOWN WITH A VENGEANCE NOT SEEN SINCE SODOM AN' GOMORRAH.

IRONIC, AS IT'S THIS DEMON WHO'LL LET ME DO IT.

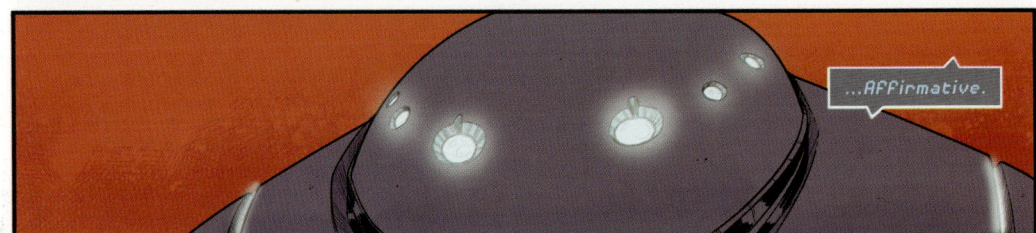

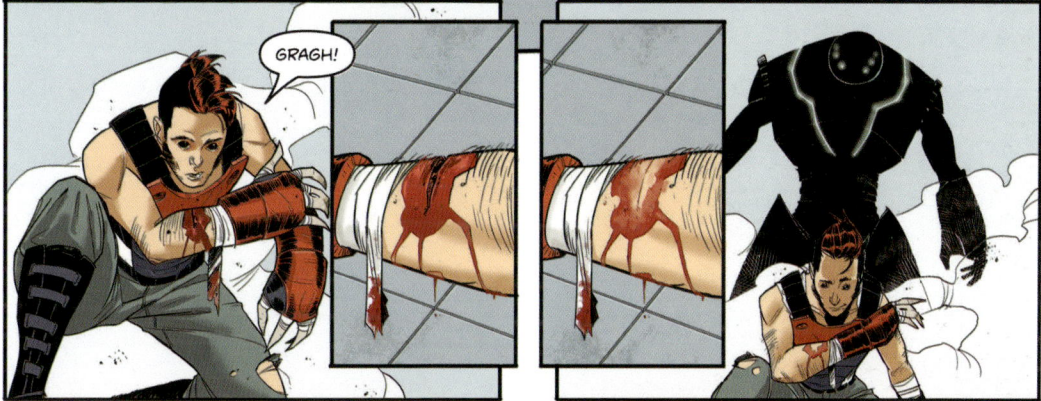

HALLELUJAH!

TO BE CONTINUED...

The Pride Issue 6 - Cover by Kris Anka

THE WORLD IS MINE.

YOU ARE MINE.

OST
...thetic powers, like some other ...ts she doesn't like talking about
...Cel Negative

FABMAN
Literally a fabulous man
X-Cel Negative

WOLF
Prowler in the night
X-Cel Negative

TWINK
Shiny and just out of bed
X-Cel Positive

MUSCLE MARY
Queen Sapphire, could beat you at anything
X-Cel Negative

...**GEL**
...st drag
...een for miles
...Cel Positive

WHITE TRASH
Tattooed bad boy with a heart of gold
X-Cel Positive

CUB
Hairy new boy
X-Cel Positive

DOES ANYONE FEEL ANY DIFFERENT?

NOPE.

I GOT NOTHIN'.

UH, GUYS...

HOW DID YOU FIGURE OUT WHERE THEY ARE?

THE SAND AT THE SCENE OF BEAR'S... BEATING.

SO?

IT WAS *DIFFERENT*, FINER THAN THE CONSTRUCTION SAND AT THE SITE, AND *MILDLY* RADIOACTIVE, ACTUALLY.

SO, IT MATCHES RECORDED SAMPLES OF SAND FOUND IN AN AREA OF THE NEW MEXICO DESERT, WHERE ATOMIC TESTS WERE CARRIED OUT *DECADES AGO*.

WHOA, WHOA, *WHOA* NOW, HONEY. RADIATION? ATOMIC?

THE RADIOACTIVITY HAS CREPT DOWN TO SAFE LEVELS NOW, JUST *SLIGHTLY* MORE THAN STANDARD BACKGROUND RADIATION.

BUT IT'S NOT THE *RADIATION* THAT WORRIES ME.

THIS GUY DOES.

HIS NAME IS REVEREND FRANKLIN PHILLIPS. HE IS AN *ACTUAL* ORDAINED MINISTER, BUT HE WAS EXCOMMUNICATED *YEARS AGO*.

HE'S A SICK MAN THAT USES RELIGION AS A WEAPON, THAT'S FOR SURE.

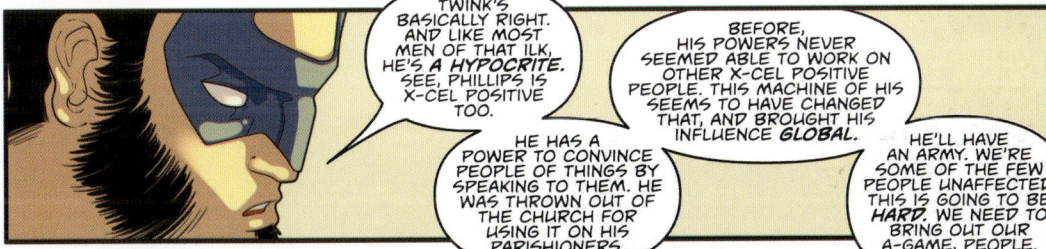

TWINK'S BASICALLY RIGHT. AND LIKE MOST MEN OF THAT ILK, HE'S *A HYPOCRITE*. SEE, PHILLIPS IS X-CEL POSITIVE TOO.

HE HAS A POWER TO CONVINCE PEOPLE OF THINGS BY SPEAKING TO THEM. HE WAS THROWN OUT OF THE CHURCH FOR USING IT ON HIS PARISHIONERS.

BEFORE, HIS POWERS NEVER SEEMED ABLE TO WORK ON OTHER X-CEL POSITIVE PEOPLE. THIS MACHINE OF HIS SEEMS TO HAVE CHANGED THAT, AND BROUGHT HIS INFLUENCE *GLOBAL*.

HE'LL HAVE AN ARMY. WE'RE SOME OF THE FEW PEOPLE UNAFFECTED. THIS IS GOING TO BE *HARD*. WE NEED TO BRING OUT OUR A-GAME, PEOPLE.

OH, HONEY, IT IS *BROUGHT!*

YOU SEE WHAT HE'S DONE TO MY DAD?

AIN'T *NO WAY* HE'S GETTIN' AWAY WITH THAT.

GOOD. THE CRUISER IS THE FASTEST JET ON THE PLANET. WE'RE NEARLY THERE.

GET READY.

136

ONE THING I *STILL* DON'T GET: WHY WEREN'T WE AFFECTED?

MY POWERS ARE SYNTHETIC, DARLING. BEST THAT MONEY CAN BUY.

RIGHT, AND WOLF IS POWERLESS. BUT I'M *X-CEL POSITIVE.* I FEEL NO DIFFERENT.

I'LL BE HONEST, TWINK, I HAVE *NO* IDEA.

BUT I DON'T MUCH CARE, LONG AS WE DESTROY THAT MACHINE AND RETRIEVE BEAR'S BODY.

WELL NOW, LITTLE SINNER, THAT MAY PROVE EASIER *SAID* THAN *DONE,* YES?

RRRRRAAARGH!

UFF!

FALL, *DAMN* YOU!

DON'T KNOW HOW.

MAYBE YOU CAN SHOW ME.

YOU-!

ME? WHAT DO YOU WANT TO DO TO ME? PLEASE, DON'T HURT ME.

YOU WOULDN'T HURT YOUR *ANGEL*, WOULD YOU? I MEAN, A *STRONG MAN* LIKE YOU, YOU GOT NOTHING TO PROVE TO ME.

HRF!

DON'T YOU *LOVE* ME, BABY?

HRF... LOVE YOU?

YEAH, WELL TOUGH LUCK, BIG BOY, I DON'T DO SUCKERS.

SUCKERS?

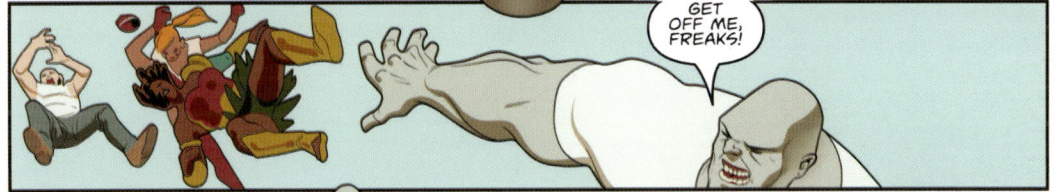

YOU'RE *SICK*, REVEREND! STOP THIS NOW!

YA THINK YOU CAN STOP MAH *WORD*! WELCOME TO THE *NEW WORLD ORDER*, FRIENDO! YOU'RE ALL DONE FOR, *YOU* AND YOUR *ILK*!

HOW DOES THAT CRAZY THING EVEN WORK, *SICKO*? IS THAT WHAT YOU WERE EXPERIMENTING ON ME FOR!

YOUNG PEOPLE TODAY! NO ONE LIKES THE IDEA OF A BIG OL' CRAZY SUPER-SCIENCE MACHINE.

EV'RYONE WANTS SOME OVERCOMPLICATED *SCI-EN-TIFIC* EXPLANATION FOR IT.

CAN'T WE LEAVE IT AT I MADE A SUPER MIND MASHER, Y'ALL?

IT'S POWERED BY THE WORD OF *"THE LORD"* HIMSELF! MAH WORD!

BUT AH DON'T EXPECT Y'ALL *SODOMITES* AND *FREAKS* TO UNNERSTAND.

GOD GAVE ME TH' BLUEPRINT O' THIS *WONDER*, SO I MIGHT SMITE TH' *WICKED*!

AN' NOW, NOW IT'S YOUR TURN TO *RETURN TO HELL*!

142

143

RAH!

HOLD! IT IS OVER.

HE IS DEFEATED.

I-- I COULDN'T STOP.

HE KILLED HARVEY... AND I... I...

HUSH, NOW.

HARVEY WOULD NOT HAVE WANTED TO MAKE YOU A KILLER.

BESIDES...

MOMENTS LATER...

DAD!

FROST, CAN YOU FREEZE *JUST* THE NON-ORGANIC ELEMENTS OF THE MACHINE? *WITHOUT* HURTING BEAR?

I CAN TRY.

I HAVE HIM!

NOW, TWINK!

CRRRAAASSH!

OH, DAD... I'M SO SORRY... I'M SO SORRY...

...WHA... F'R...?

146

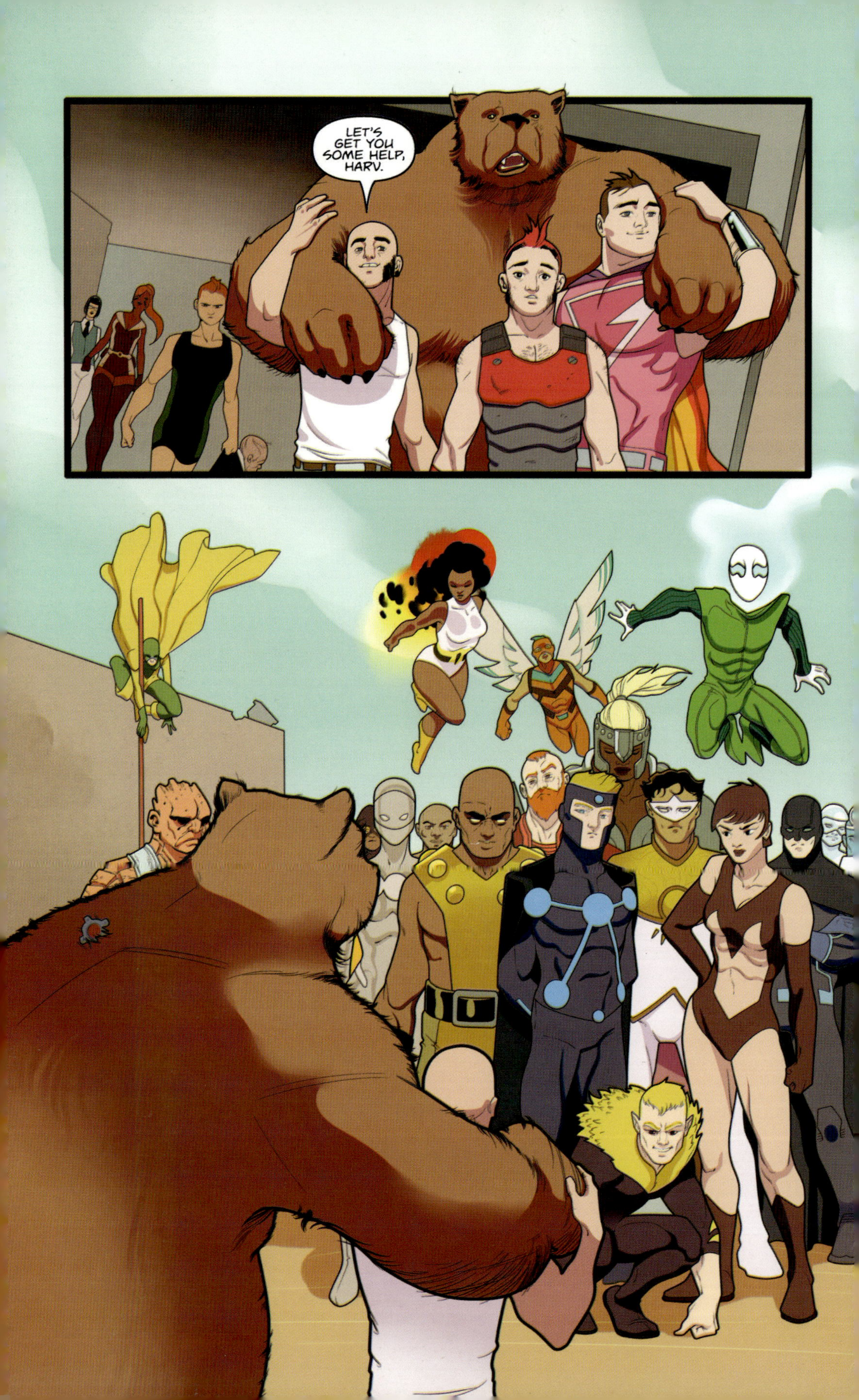
LET'S GET YOU SOME HELP, HARV.

YEEEEEEEEEAAAAH!

WELL NOW, FABS... THIS FEELIN' *ABOUT RIGHT?*

IT'S BEEN **TWO MONTHS** SINCE THE WORLD DOMINATION ATTEMPT BY **THE REVEREND.**

THWARTED BY THE WORLD'S **NEWEST** AND **MOST DIFFERENT** SUPERHERO TEAM, THE PRIDE.

LATER TODAY, THE PRIDE WILL BE MEETING THE PRESIDENT OF THE UNITED STATES TO RECEIVE AN HONOUR FOR THEIR **VALIANT WORK** IN STOPPING THE MADMAN.

AND I FOR ONE COULD NOT BE **PROUDER** TO SAY THAT **I BELIEVE IN THE PRIDE!**

...BASHER **STILL AT LARGE.** THOUGH REPORTEDLY **GRIEVOUSLY WOUNDED** IN BATTLE, **NO BODY** WAS FOUND AT SCENE...

...WORLD OWES A **MASSIVE** DEBT TO **THE PRIDE,** WHO'S TIRELESS EFFORTS TO IMPROVE REPRESENTATION FOR LGBT...

...JUSTICE DIVISION ADMITTED THEY ONCE ENACTED A **'DON'T ASK, DON'T TELL'** POLICY, WHICH THEY HAVE NOW **REMOVED** FROM THEIR CHARTER...

HI BILLY. GUYS.

O.M.G... FABMAN! YOU'RE SO AWESOME!

CAN I GET A SELFIE WITH YOU?

SURE, JUST LET ME HAVE A QUICK WORD WITH MY FRIEND, BILLY.

152

YOU DID IT, THEN. YOU SAVED THE WORLD.

SURE DID, KIDDO. AND I COULDN'T HAVE DONE IT WITHOUT YOUR INSPIRATION.

HERE. I GOT THIS TO THANK YOU, BILLY.

OH MY GOD, THANK YOU, FABMAN!

I WANT YOU TO HAVE THIS. Y'KNOW, TO REMIND YOU.

BILLY, I COULDN'T...

IT'LL REMIND YOU THAT YOU CAME A LONG WAY, AND YOU FOUGHT A HARD FIGHT, AND... WELL, AND...

AND NOW EVERYONE SEES YOU AS THE HERO YOU ARE. JUST LIKE I ALWAYS DID.

THANK YOU, BILLY.

153

written by **JOE GLASS**

pencils by **MAXIME GARBARINI**

inks & colours by **HECTOR BARROS**

letters by **MIKE STOCK**

RUNNING ORDER

IT GETS BETTER

Written by Joe Glass, Art and Letters by Gavin Mitchell, Colors by Kris Carter

RIDE THE PAIN

Written by Joe Glass, Art by Samir Barrett, Letters by Mike Stock

IN THIS SHIRT

Story by Joe Glass, Lyrics by Jaime McDermott and The Irrepressibles, Art by Joshua Faith, Colors by Kris Carter, Letters by Mike Stock

THE PRIDE VS. THE PRIDE

Written by PJ Montgomery, Art by Chris Wildgoose, Colors by Ben Wilsonham, Letters by Mike Stock

MOVING FORWARD

Written by Joe Glass, Art by Denis Medri, Colors by Ben Wilsonham, Letters by Mike Stock

LADIES NIGHT

Written by Joe Glass, Art by Dani Abram, Letters by Mike Stock

A DETECTIVE CALLS

Written by Joe Glass, Art by Joshua Faith, Colors by Ben Wilsonham, Letters by Mike Stock

OUTRAGE

Written by Joe Glass, Layouts by Cory Smith and JD Faith, Art by JD Faith, Colors by Ben Wilsonham, Letters by Mike Stock

YOU CAN'T GO HOME AGAIN

Written by Joe Glass, Art by Martin Kirby, Colors by Ben Wilsonham, Letters by Mike Stock

THE MORNING AFTER

Written by Joe Glass, Art by Adam Graphite, Letters by Mike Stock

OH, NO SHE BETTER DON'T

Written by Joe Glass, Art by Gavin Mitchell, Letters by Mike Stock

GUN MACHINE

Written by Joe Glass, Art by Andy W Clift, Colors by Ben Wilsonham, Letters by Mike Stock

OPEN UP

Written by Joe Glass, Art by Tana Ford, Colors by Ben Wilsonham, Letters by Mike Stock

MILKSHAKE

Written by Mike Garley, Art by Chris Imber, Colors by Ben Wilsonham, Letters by Mike Stock

COME TOGETHER

Written by Joe Glass, Art by Andy Bennett, Letters by Mike Stock

THE PACK

Written by Joe Glass, Art by Ben Wilsonham, Letters by Mike Stock

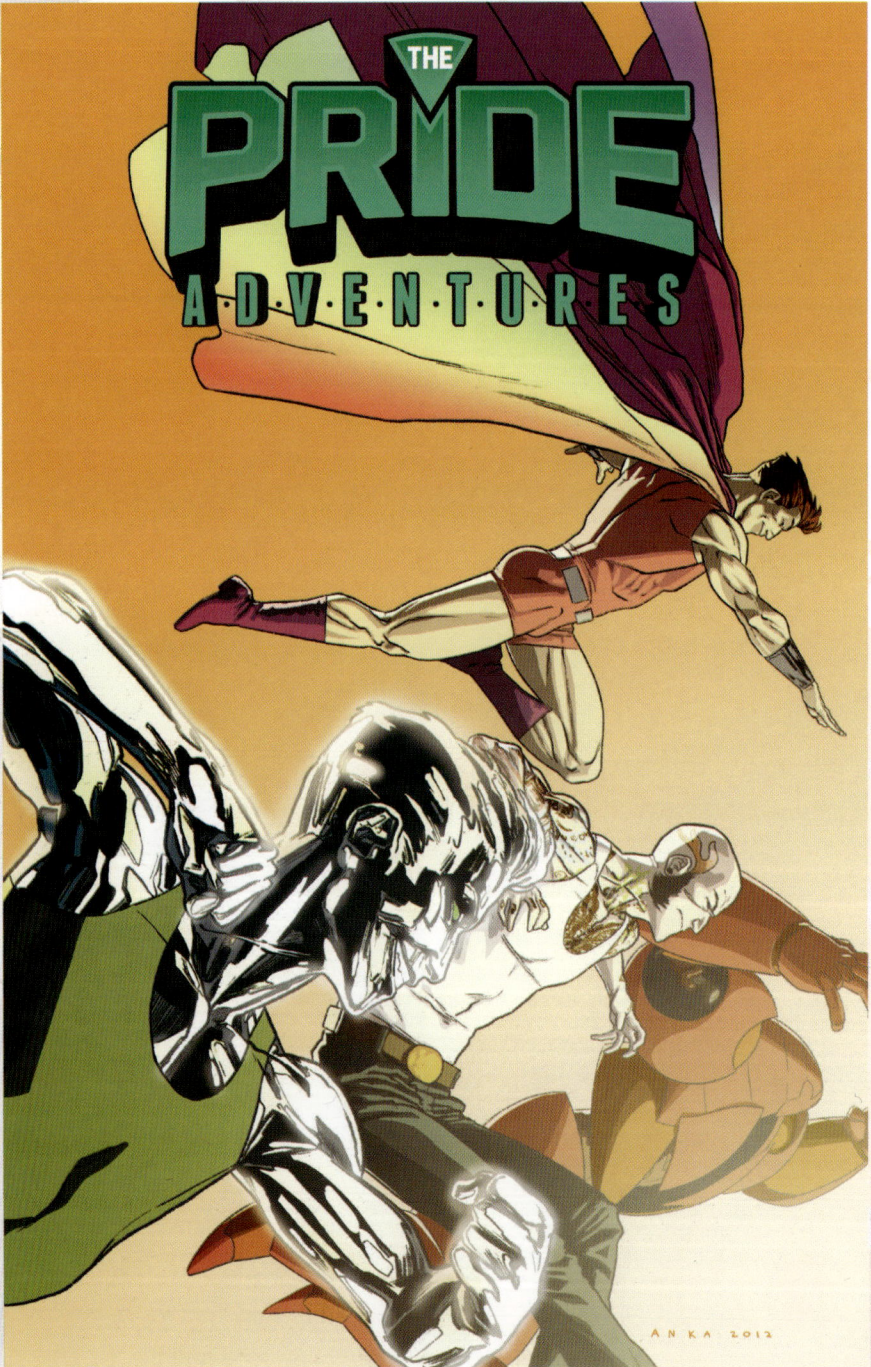

The Pride Adventures Issue 1 - Cover by Kris Anka

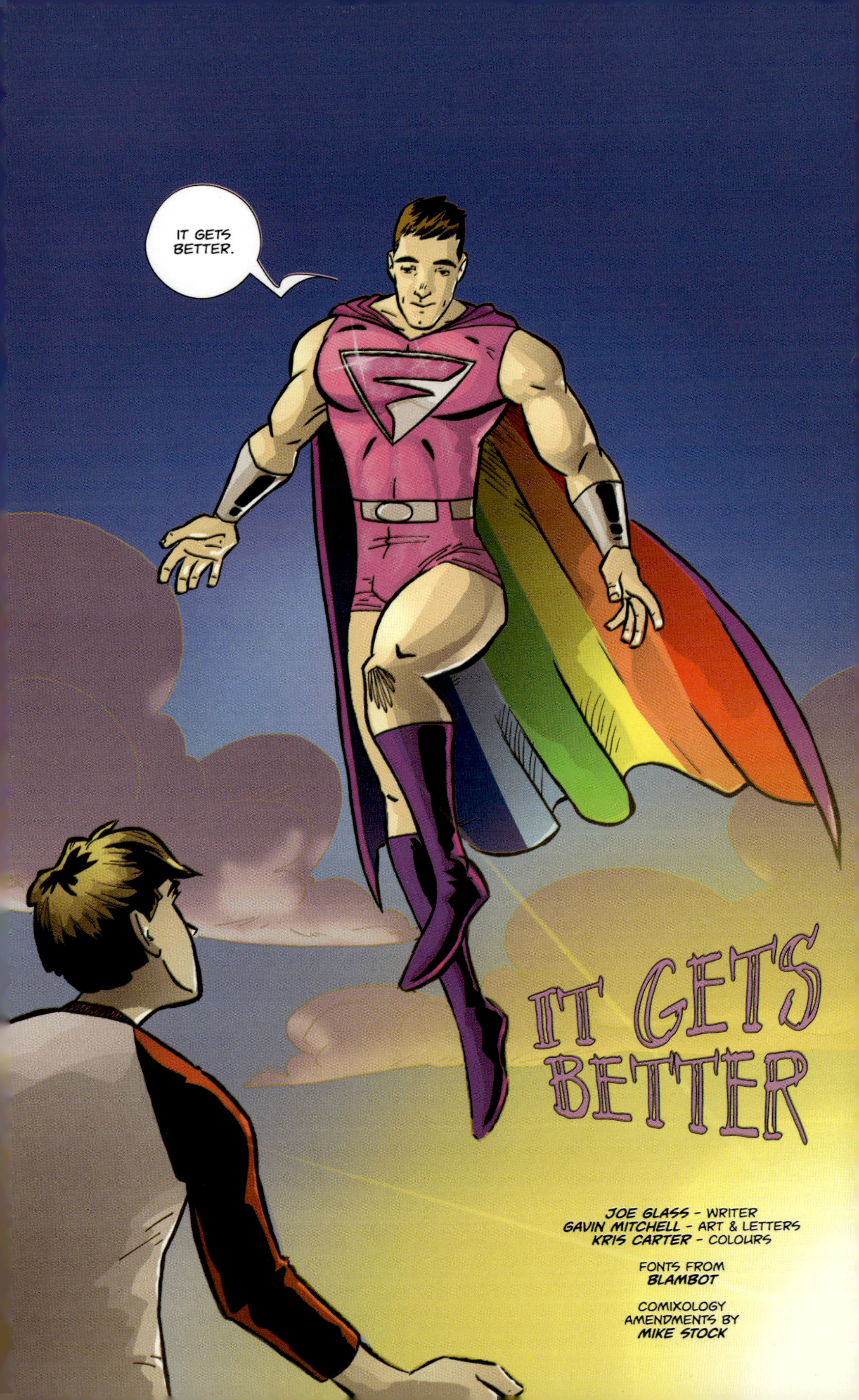
IT GETS BETTER.
IT GETS BETTER
JOE GLASS - WRITER
GAVIN MITCHELL - ART & LETTERS
KRIS CARTER - COLOURS
FONTS FROM BLAMBOT
COMIXOLOGY AMENDMENTS BY MIKE STOCK

NOT YOU! THERE COULDN'T POSSIBLY BE A WORSE A PERSON TO COME AND 'SAVE' ME!

÷SIGH÷ I GET THAT A LOT.

LOOK, KID, WHATEVER IT IS, I'M SURE IT'S NOT THAT BAD...

NOT THAT BAD? THEY KNOW! DAMMIT, THEY CAUGHT ME WITH HIM, AND THEY'RE GOING TO TELL EVERYONE AND... AND... THEY KNOW I'M GAY!

THEY'RE GOING TO RUIN ME. MY LIFE... MY LIFE IS OVER...

OH.

OH HONEY, I'M SO SORRY. BUT THIS ISN'T THE WAY TO SOLVE THIS. IT'S REALLY NOT, BELIEVE ME...

DON'T! I KNOW WHAT YOU'RE GOING TO SAY, THAT I HAVE SO MUCH TO LIVE FOR, AND THAT I SHOULD FACE THIS ALL HEAD ON, BUT IT'S CRAP!

MY LIFE IS RUINED. MY FRIENDS... MY FRIENDS WILL HATE ME, MY FAMILY... THEY... THEY WON'T LOVE ME ANYMORE... YOU DON'T KNOW ANYTHING!

YOU'RE RIGHT. I AM GOING TO TELL YOU ALL THOSE THINGS, AND THEY'RE TRUE, SWEETIE, TRUST ME...

AND MAYBE I WON'T KNOW EXACTLY HOW THINGS WILL HAPPEN OR WHEN, BUT I KNOW THEY'LL IMPROVE...

BUT YOU'RE WRONG ABOUT ONE THING. IT WASN'T ALWAYS EASY FOR ME... AND I DO KNOW WHERE YOU ARE RIGHT NOW.

I'VE SEEN YOU ON THE NEWS, SO PROUD AND FLYING YOUR FLAG... WELL, IT MUSTA BEEN SO EASY FOR YOU, BUT THAT'S NOT ME, DUDE!

BECAUSE I WAS HERE MYSELF WHEN I WAS NOT MUCH YOUNGER THAN YOU.

161

I ALWAYS KNEW THAT I WAS DIFFERENT, BUT THAT DOESN'T MEAN IT WAS ALWAYS EASY FOR ME.

THE WORST PART WAS EVERYONE ELSE KNEW I WAS DIFFERENT TOO...

...AND THE GUYS ON THE FOOTBALL TEAM PUT TWO AND TWO TOGETHER AND FOR THE FIRST TIME IN THEIR LIVES GOT IT RIGHT.

THAT MADE IT WORSE IN A WAY. IT FELT LIKE I HAD A DIRTY LITTLE SECRET AND EVERYONE KNEW IT, AND I WAS ALMOST DESERVING ALL THIS.

I STILL HADN'T COME TO LOVE AND RESPECT MYSELF, AND SO I DIDN'T HAVE THE STRENGTH TO STAND UP FOR MYSELF.

FAGGOT

I COULDN'T SEE HOW ANYONE'S LIFE COULD BE ANY WORSE THAN MINE. AND THAT'S WHEN I THOUGHT 'WHY BOTHER?'

AND SO I CAME HERE...

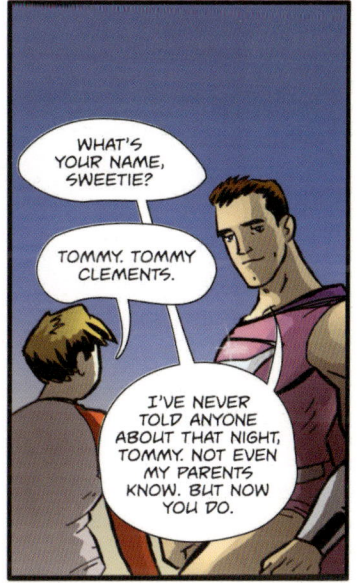

TEEN GAY SUICIDE

AND IN TEXAS TODAY, BILLY CARDONI WAS FOUND DEAD AFTER HAVING TAKEN A LETHAL DOSE OF PRESCRIPTION PAINKILLERS IN A SADLY SUCCESSFUL SUICIDE ATTEMPT. THE BOY REPORTEDLY COMMITTED SUICIDE OVER ALLEGED HOMOPHOBIC BULLYING AT HIS SCHOOL IN AUSTIN, TEXAS. BILLY'S PARENTS ARE 'INCONSOLABLE' AT THE LOSS OF THEIR SON, DESCRIBED BY FRIENDS AND FAMILY AS 'EXUBERANT, HAPPY AND FULL OF LIFE'.

HE WAS JUST THIRTEEN YEARS OF AGE.

OH GOD...

ABRAHAM LINCOLN HIGH SCHOOL

BROOKLYN, NEW YORK

OH GOD, TOMMY! I'M SO GLAD YOU'RE OKAY!

YEAH, MAN. BUT, DUDE, WE'RE YOUR FRIENDS... AND YOU'RE THE SAME GUY YOU ALWAYS WERE.

IF ANYONE GIVES YOU ANY TROUBLE...

TOM, DUDE, NO ONE CARES, REALLY. THOSE TOOLS WENT WAY TOO FAR.

IT'S OKAY. I GOT YOU GUYS. IT'LL BE TOUGH SOMETIMES...

...BUT IT GETS BETTER, DUDE.

THANK YOU.

IF YOU EVER FEEL LIKE YOU NEED TO TALK TO SOMEONE; LIKE THE WORLD IS TOO TOUGH AND YOU JUST WANT SOMEONE TO LISTEN TO YOU FOR A CHANGE.

PLEASE DON'T HESITATE TO CONTACT ONE OF THESE WONDERFUL ORGANISATIONS. THE GOOD MEN AND WOMEN THERE CARE ABOUT YOU, AND WANT TO HEAR FROM YOU.

IN THE US: CONTACT THE TREVOR PROJECT ON 866-4-U-TREVOR (866-488-7386)

IN THE UK: CONTACT CHILDLINE ON 0800 11 11 OR GO TO www.childline.org.uk OR www.stonewall.org.uk

AND HEAR MESSAGES FROM ACROSS THE WORLD AT: www.itgetsbetter.org

RIDE THE PAIN

I'M GONNA KNOCK YOU ONTO YOUR SHINY, METAL @$$!!

RIDE THE PAIN
STORY **JOE GLASS**
ART **SAMIR BARRETT**
LETTERS **MIKE STOCK**

THAT ACTUALLY KINDA HURT.

PLENTY MORE WHERE THAT CAME FROM!

WELL, I GUESS I BETTER COME AN' GET IT, HUH?

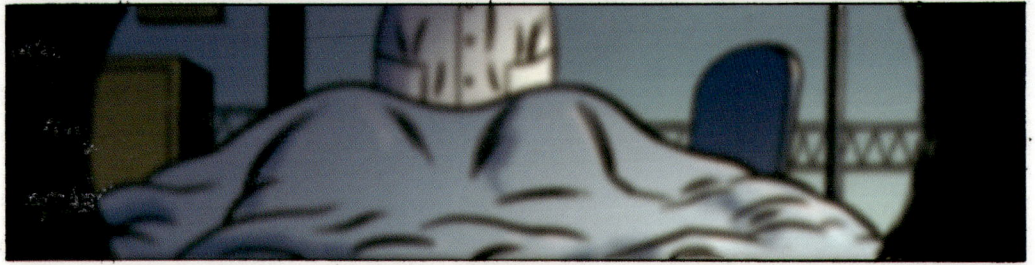

I AM LOST.

IN OUR RAINBOW,
NOW OUR RAINBOW...

...IS GONE.

OVERCAST, BY
YOUR SHADOW.

AS OUR WORLD'S
MOVE ON.

IN THIS SHIRT

I CAN BE YOU...TO BE
NEAR YOU...FOR A WHILE...

IN THIS SHIRT, I CAN BE
YOU, TO BE NEAR YOU.

FOR A WHILE.

171

THERE'S A CRANE, KNOCKING DOWN

ALL THESE THINGS

THAT WE WERE.

I AWAKE

IN THE NIGHT

TO HEAR THE ENGINES PURR.

THERE'S A PAIN, IT DOES RIPPLE

THROUGH MY FRAME ...MAKES ME LAME.

THERE'S A THORN, IN MY SIDE

IT'S THE SHAPE, IT'S THE PRIDE

OF YOU AND ME, EVER CHANGING, MOVING ON NOW...MOVING FAST

AND HIS TOUCH, MUST BE WANTING

MUST BECOME FREE TO ACT

BUT I NEED

NEED TO TELL YOU, THAT I LOVE YOU, IT NEVER RESTS

AND I'VE BLED, EVERY DAY NOW

FOR A YEAR, FOR A YEAR

174

175

TO THE DEPTHS OF THE SOIL

BURIED DEEP IN THE GROUND

ON THE WIND, I COULD HEAR YOU

CALL MY NAME, HELD THE SOUNDS

I AM LOST

I AM LOST, IN OUR RAINBOW, NOW OUR RAINBOW IS GONE

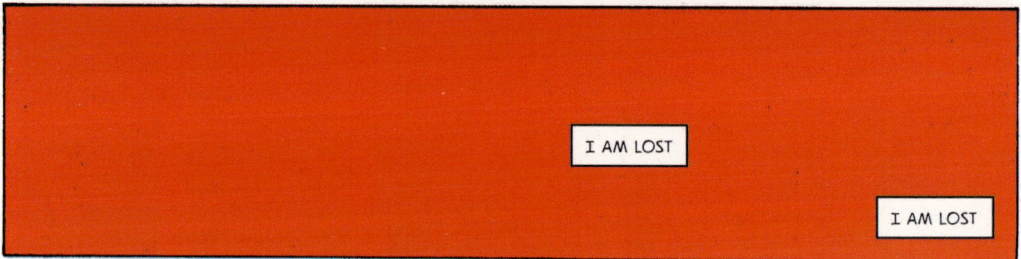

I AM LOST, IN OUR RAINBOW, NOW OUR RAINBOW IS GONE.

I AM LOST

I AM LOST

I AM LOST.

LEWIS MARTELL
And Jai
OUTRAGE
A HERO TO MANY
Wing

IN THIS SHIRT

Story by JOE GLASS, lyrics by JAMIE MCDERMOTT and THE IRREPRESSIBLES.

Art by JOSHUA FAITH, colours by KRIS CARTER, letters by MIKE STOCK

THE IRREPRESSIBLES ALBUM IS AVAILABLE AT: HTTP://GOO.GL/YAZSV

The Pride Adventures Issue 2 - Cover by W Scott Forbes

LIVE

THE **ONGOING** SPATE OF BANK ROBBERIES IN THE CITY CONTINUED THIS MORNING, AS THE **GRIFFIN BANK** FOUND ITSELF THE **LATEST TARGET.**

THE THIEVES **ESCAPED** THE SCENE WITH **FIVE MILLION DOLLARS** IN CASH, LEAVING **FOUR** PEOPLE WOUNDED. ONE MAN IS IN **CRITICAL** CONDITION.

NEWS

LIVE

THE GROUP RESPONSIBLE FOR THE CRIMES, WHO HAVE SO FAR **EVADED CAPTURE** BY THE AUTHORITIES, **APPEAR** TO BE SETTING THEMSELVES UP AS A NEW **SUPERVILLAIN TEAM,** AND HAVE INDICATED THAT THEY **WILL** BE STRIKING AGAIN, POSSIBLY AS SOON AS THIS AFTERNOON.

CALLING THEMSELVES-

NEWS

THE **PRIDE!**

YOU **COWER** BEFORE US LIKE **MEWLING, BABY ZEBRAS.** WE ARE THE **TOP** OF THE FOOD CHAIN, AND **YOU** ARE OUR **PREY.**

WE WILL SOON TAKE **OUR RIGHTFUL** PLACES AS **RULERS** OF THIS CITY. **ALL** WILL BOW BENEATH US, IN **AWE** OF OUR **MAJESTY!**

HONEY, I DON'T KNOW WHAT'S **WORSE...**

179

THE PRIDE VS. THE PRIDE

WRITTEN BY PJ MONTGOMERY
ART BY CHRIS WILDGOOSE
COLOURS BY BEN WILSONHAM
LETTERS BY MIKE STOCK

183

END.

SAN FRANCISCO IS THE **LEADING** FINANCIAL AND CULTURAL CENTRE FOR THE NORTHERN CALIFORNIAN AREA.

IT HAS SEEN **MANY** INCREDIBLE THINGS, FROM THE **PROGRESSION OF HUMAN RIGHTS,** MEN AND WOMEN **STANDING TALL** TO SPREAD MESSAGES OF **PEACE** AND **TOGETHERNESS...**

IT HAS ALSO SEEN **TERRIBLE** AND **DEVASTATING** THINGS.

ISLANDS WHERE THE **CONDEMNED** WERE **SHIPPED AWAY, OBLITERATING** NATURAL DISASTERS...

AND **NOW,** AN **INVASION FORCE** UNLIKE **ANY** IT HAS SEEN BEFORE.

AREN'T YOU GLAD I CALLED REINFORCEMENTS NOW, HONEY?

COME NOW, **DARLING.** WE COULD HAVE HANDLED THIS OURSELVES, I'M SURE.

MOVING FORWARD

WRITTEN BY *JOE GLASS* ART BY *DENIS MEDRI* COLOURS BY *BEN WILSONHAM* LETTERS BY *MIKE STOCK*

TRAITOR! HOW *DARE* YOU STILL CALL YOURSELF *OUR* QUEEN!

YOU *ABANDONED US* FOR THESE... *THESE ANIMALS!*

WHEN I LEFT, MY PEOPLE WERE *SAFE, SECURE* AND STRONG IN OUR WAYS OF *PEACE.*

THESE PEOPLE *NEEDED* ME, AND *NEED* ME STILL.

ALAS, IT WOULD APPEAR *MY OWN PEOPLE* NEED ME ALSO. I HAD THOUGHT I LEFT THEM IN *BETTER* HANDS.

RRRAAA- AAARRRH!

ATTACK!

YOU *LEFT US!* FOR THESE *NEANDERTHALS!*

YOU *ABANDONED YOUR SISTERS!* WAS IT *WORTH IT?* FOR THE *HATEFUL WARMONGERS* OF MAN?

YOU HAVE BEEN *MISLED*, SISTERS.

I SAW YOU *FIGHT*, BUT YOUR *HEARTS* WERE NOT IN IT, BUT YOU *DARE NOT* DISOBEY YOUR *REGENT* AND *SISTER*, *MEDEA*.

I APOLOGISE FOR LEAVING YOU FOR *SO LONG*.

BUT UNTIL NOW, YOU *DID NOT NEED ME*. THE REST OF THE WORLD DID.

OUR WAYS HAVE NEVER BEEN *CONQUEST*. UNTIL I CAME TO THESE LANDS, WE KEPT *OURSELVES* TO *OURSELVES*.

BUT THIS IS *WRONG*.

THEY HAVE MADE *GREAT STEPS* ALREADY.

BUT THEY HAVE *MANY MORE* TO GO. WE *MUST* BE AN EXAMPLE TO THEM, NOT A STICK TO *BEAT* THEM TOWARDS THEIR FUTURE.

WE WILL TAKE THE *SMALL* STEPS TO THAT FUTURE... *TOGETHER!*

END.

191

WRITTEN BY JOE GLASS
ART BY DANI ABRAM
LETTERS BY MIKE STOCK
DEAR ONE, YOU HAVE A STRONG BUILD FOR A WOMAN OF MAN'S LAND.
PERHAPS YOU COULD SHOW ME YOUR TRAINING REGIME?
OH, HONEY, I GOT MORE THAN YOU WOULD WANT T'SEE.
DRINK AND BE MERRY!
LADIES NIGHT
SWEET FROST, WHAT IS IT THE PEOPLE OF THIS LAND SAY?
WHY THE LONG MOUTH?
FACE, DEAR, FACE. BUT CLOSE ENOUGH.
I WAS JUST CONTEMPLATING ON HOW IMPOSSIBLE IT IS TO FIND A DECENT COCKTAIL ON THIS DAMNED COLONY.
AND NOTHING IS ANYWHERE NEAR COLD ENOUGH FOR ME.
AND HONESTLY, WHO SERVES A MOJITO IN A MARTIN-
RRMMBB

TREMBLE, *FOOLS!*

OH, *WHAT* NOW!

BOW BEFORE THE *MASTER* OF THE WATERS, *AQUALORD!*

I CONTROL THE *TIDES*, THE *SEAS, EVERY DROP OF MOIST—*

AAAAND THAT'S *QUITE* ENOUGH OF *THAT*, DEAR.

-KIK!

WELL, *THAT* WAS KINDA *ANTI-CLIMACTIC*... I DIDN'T EVEN GET TO THROW SOME SHADE.

DARLING, IT'S BEEN QUITE A *TEDIOUS* DAY ALREADY, AND THE MONOLOGUING VILLAINS ARE *OVERLY DREARY.*

BESIDES, DEAR, I *REALLY* NEEDED THE ICE.

PLIP

END.

A DETECTIVE CALLS

WRITTEN BY **JOE GLASS**
ART BY **JOSHUA FAITH**
COLOURS BY **BEN WILSONHAM**
LETTERS BY **MIKE STOCK**

WE NEED YOUR HELP.

THIS GUY'S GOING AROUND IN A *GIANT* SUIT OF ARMOUR AND HE'S PULLING PEOPLE APART.

IN ONE CASE, *LITERALLY.*

HE'S CALLING HIMSELF *OUTRAGE*, BUT HE'S NOT THE ORIGINAL GUY. HIM WE *LIKED.* THIS GUY...

THIS GUY'S A *KILLER.*

YEAH, FROM WHAT WE HEARD, HE'S KILLING *GAY BASHERS* AND *HOMOPHOBES.*

GOOD RIDDANCE TO *BAD TRASH,* HONEY.

ANGEL!

I HAVE A QUESTION: WHERE DID THIS GUY GET *ALL* THE TOOLS AND EQUIPMENT HE NEEDED TO MAKE THE SUIT? I MEAN, *IT LOOKS* KINDA COMPLEX.

WING IS A FORMER EMPLOYEE OF WILDE INDUSTRIES.

HE WAS A *HIGH UP* IN EXPERIMENTAL TECHNOLOGIES, *SPECIALISING* IN BODY ARMOURS AND TOOLS FOR *EXTREME SITUATIONS.*

OH.

I'M SORRY, HONEY, BUT I *STILL* DON'T SEE WHY WE SHOULD STOP HIM. HE'S NOT HURTING ANYONE WHO DON'T DESERVE IT.

AND NO WORSE THAN ANYTHING *THEY'VE* DONE T'OTHERS...

ME 'N' BEAR GOT CALLED WHILE PATROLLING ONCE. A GAY KID WAS BEING *BEATEN UP* UNDER A BRIDGE IN CENTRAL PARK.

WE RAN, *FASTER* THAN I THINK I *EVER* RUN BEFORE.

BUT WE WERE *TOO* LATE.

KID WAS *BARELY RECOGNISABLE.* THEY *WOULDN'T* EVEN LET HIS *MAMMA* SEE HIM, STATE HE WAS IN.

LISTEN, *I UNDERSTAND*, BUT THIS MONSTER *NEEDS* TO BE STOPPED.

AND IT'S *NOT* JUST THE VICTIMS OF HIS *OWN* ATTACKS HE'S HURT NOW EITHER.

THE KID HE WAS *'SAVING'* IN HIS LAST ATTACK...

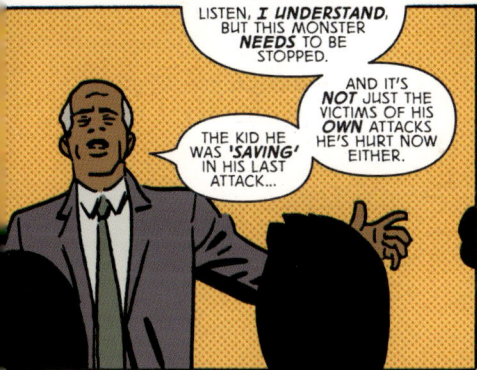

KID WAS *SAT* THERE, WATCHING AS THIS *MONSTROSITY* CAME LIKE A *BAT OUTTA HELL* AND PUT THE BEAT DOWN ON A MAN LIKE *NOTHIN'* BEFORE.

SURE, THE GUY HAD BEEN *KICKING* HIM IN THE GUT ONLY *MOMENTS* BEFORE, BUT HE WAS *MORE* SCARED OF THIS *HULKING* BEAST, I IMAGINE.

HE *EVEN* HAD TO WATCH A MAN GET *RIPPED* IN TWO... HEARD THE SOUND OF HIS SKIN AND BONE *TEARIN'*...

I SAY *'IMAGINE'* 'CAUSE THE KID HASN'T MADE A SOUND SINCE THAT NIGHT. HE'S TOO *TERRIFIED* TO LEAVE HIS BED.

OUTRAGE HAS *DESTROYED* HIM JUST AS *BADLY* AS HE DID THE KIDS' ATTACKER.

197

HOW **LONG** BEFORE HE STARTS KILLING WITNESSES? WHETHER BY ACCIDENT **OR** ON PURPOSE.

AND **NEXT** TIME—

STOP. WE'RE ON IT, DETECTIVE WILLIAMS.

YES, **DARLING.** LIKE THEM OR NOT, NO ONE **DESERVES** TO BE SUMMARILY **ENDED** IN SUCH A **GRISLY** MANNER.

I'M **HAPPY** TO PUNISH THOSE THAT **DESERVE IT,** BUT THERE **MUST ALWAYS** BE A LINE.

FIIIIIINE! SO, WHAT'S THE PLAN, **BIG GUY?**

GOOD. WE HAVE A GUY IN CUSTODY, BEAT UP **THREE** GAY KIDS WITH A **GANG OF THUGS** TWO WEEKS AGO.

IT'S HIS **SECOND** OFFENSE. WE'RE GONNA LET HIM OFF ON A TECHNICALITY.

AH, **BAIT.** HOW DELIGHTFULLY DEVIOUS.

THANKS. WE'VE, SHALL WE SAY, **SURREPTITIOUSLY** TAGGED THE GUY. WE WANT **YOU** TO KEEP AN EYE ON HIM, WAIT FOR **OUTRAGE** TO SHOW UP. YOU IN?

WE'LL BE READY.

The Pride Adventures Issue 3 - Cover by Jamal Campbell

SO, DO WE THINK THIS IS GOING TO WORK?

NO WAY OF KNOWING 'TIL WE TRY.

PERHAPS THE QUESTION IS: DO WE *WANT IT TO?*

WHAT HE'S DOING IS WRONG.

IT'S MURDER.

DID YOU KNOW HIM? THIS GUY IN THE ARMOR, I MEAN?

DIDN'T THE DETECTIVE SAY HE WAS AN EMPLOYEE OF YOURS?

MURDERING VIOLENT MEN, THOUGH.

BUT YOU ARE RIGHT. THERE IS NO HONOR IN HIS ACTIONS. ONLY ANGER.

I THINK I MET HIM BRIEFLY, WHEN HE WAS FIRST HIRED. BUT I READ HIS FILE.

KID'S A *GENIUS,* WORKING ON ALL KINDS OF MILITARY PROJECTS FOR US.

MILITARY?

DEFENSE STUFF... HE'S MADE SOME ALTERATIONS.

I READ RECENT EMPLOYEE EVALUATION REPORTS.

SINCE HIS PARTNER WAS KILLED IN THE GAY BASHING, ONCE HE CAME BACK TO WORK AFTER THE HOSPITAL, JAI WING CHANGED.

PREVIOUSLY, A GREAT GUY, FRIENDLY, TEAM PLAYER. HE TURNED AGGRESSIVE, DISTANT AND A LONER.

THAT MUST BE WHEN HE STARTED STEALING EQUIPMENT FROM WILDE INDUSTRIES.

ACTUALLY... I KNEW HIS PARTNER.

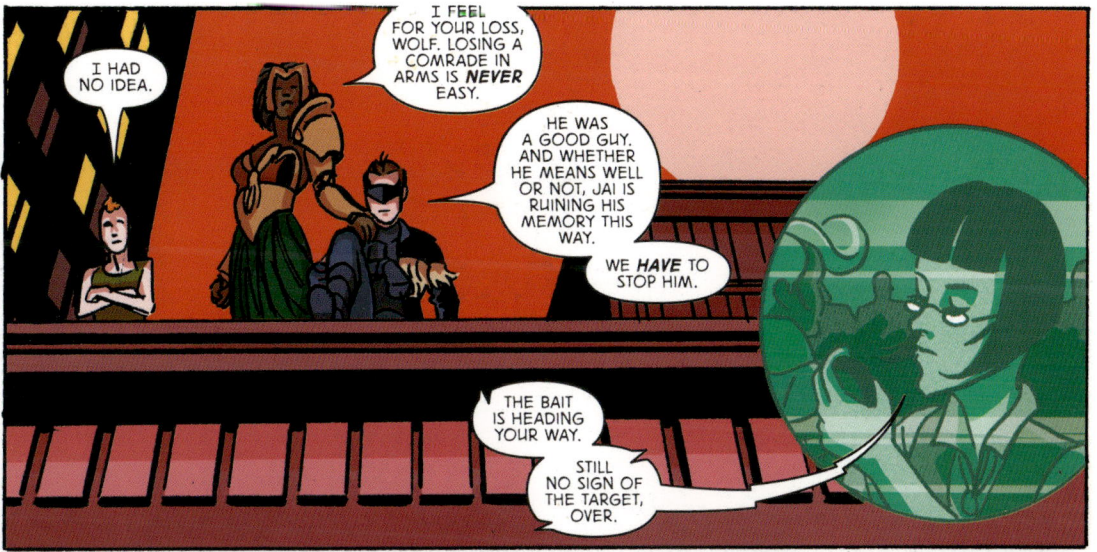

I HAD NO IDEA.

I FEEL FOR YOUR LOSS, WOLF. LOSING A COMRADE IN ARMS IS *NEVER* EASY.

HE WAS A GOOD GUY. AND WHETHER HE MEANS WELL OR NOT, JAI IS RUINING HIS MEMORY THIS WAY.

WE *HAVE* TO STOP HIM.

THE BAIT IS HEADING YOUR WAY. STILL NO SIGN OF THE TARGET, OVER.

OKAY, GUYS, GET READY. WHEN OUR MARK ENTERS THE ALLEY, HE'S *VULNERABLE.*

CAN'T SAY I CARE HOW VULNERABLE HE IS, SUGAR.

LISTEN, ANGEL, HE'LL BE GOING *STRAIGHT* BACK TO JAIL WHEN THIS IS DONE. WE HAVE TO CATCH OUTRAGE AND *STOP* THIS CARNAGE.

DUNNO WHY I AGREED TO THIS. DAMN FOOLS GONNA GET ME *KILLED.*

AIN'T *NO WAY* THEY'LL BE KEEPING THEIR PROMISES. I'M GOING TO JAIL *NO MATTER* WHAT.

LEAST THERE I'D BE *ALIVE.*

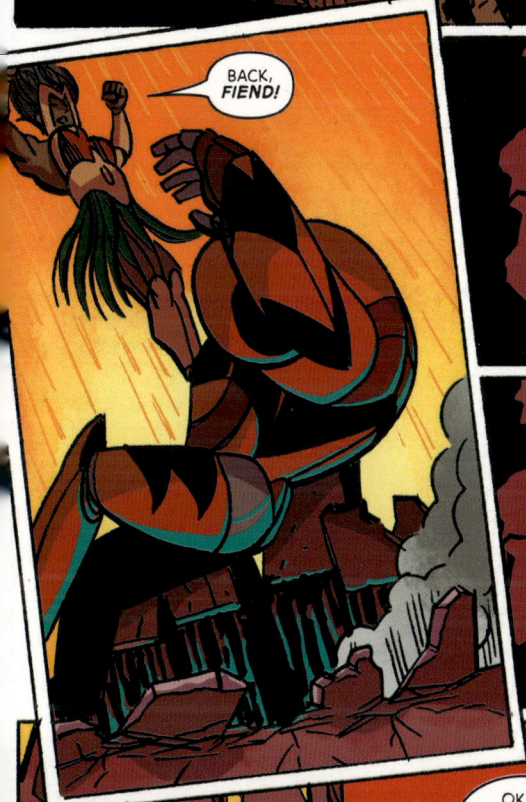

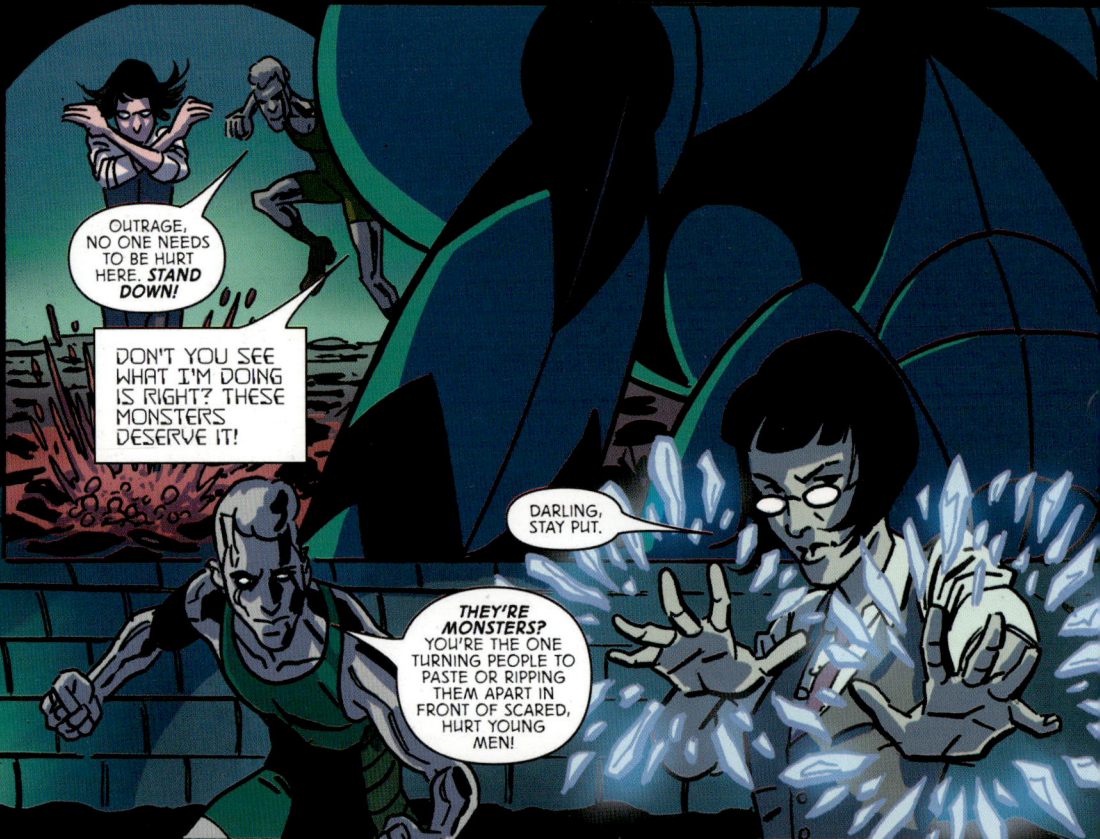

MAYBE ANYONE WHO FIGHTS TO PROTECT THESE MONSTERS ARE MONSTERS THEMSELVES.

MAYBE I SHOULD BE BRANCHING OUT...

STOP!

JAI, PLEASE... THIS ISN'T YOU. AND IT CERTAINLY ISN'T ME.

LEWIS?!

THAT'S RIGHT, BABY. IT'S ME... I'VE MISSED YOU.

BUT WHAT YOU'RE DOING, IT AIN'T RIGHT. YOU'VE *GOT* TO STOP THIS.

I DID IT FOR *YOU*. TO HONOR YOU, SO YOUR NAME LIVED ON.

BUT THIS IS *NEVER* WHAT I WANTED. I WAS *NEVER* A KILLER.

BUT THEY KILLED YOU. THEY *HAD* TO PAY.

BUT THAT ISN'T YOUR RIGHT TO DECIDE.

GAH!

HOLY S@%!

NOT MY RIGHT?! **THEY KILLED HIM!** TOOK HIM AWAY FROM ME!

WHO ARE YOU TO TALK ABOUT RIGHTS, USING THE IMAGE OF MY OWN **DEAD LOVER** AGAINST ME!

AND WHAT ABOUT **YOU?** USING HIS IMAGE TO TAINT HIS MEMORY.

WHAT?!

I KNEW OUTRAGE. HE WAS A **DAMN** GOOD MAN. AND HE KNEW WHERE THE LINE WAS DRAWN.

HE **NEVER** CROSSED IT.

BUT YOU'VE TAKEN HIS NAME, HIS **GOOD WORK,** AND CROSS THAT LINE. **EVERY SINGLE TIME** YOU TAINT HIS NAME.

IF YOU WON'T THINK ABOUT HOW HE **NEVER** WANTED THIS LIFE FOR YOU, AT **LEAST** DON'T KEEP DISHONORING HIS MEMORY **THIS WAY.**

I... I DON'T...

I MEAN, I WEAR THIS... TO BE CLOSE TO HIM... I...

NAY, WOLF. DIPLOMACY SHALL BE MADE ONLY WHEN WE STAND ON *EQUAL* FOOTING.

NO LONGER SHALL WE PARLAY WITH WALKING WEAPONS OF MURDER. WE WANT NOT THE MACHINE, WE WANT *THE MAN!*

RRRRRRRRRR RRRRRRRRBZZ Z0-01010---

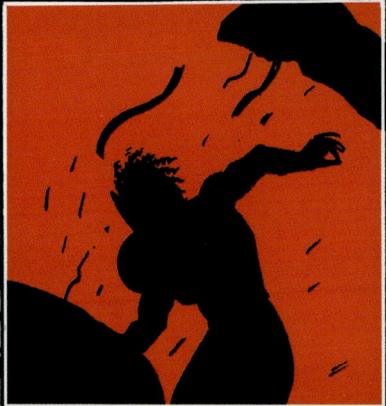

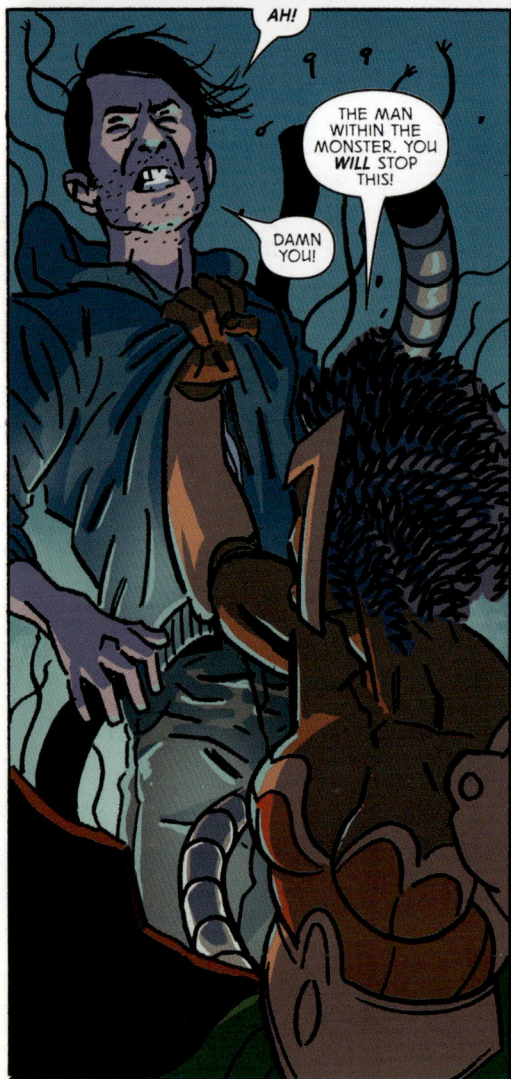

AH!

THE MAN WITHIN THE MONSTER. YOU *WILL* STOP THIS!

DAMN YOU!

JAI, I'M SORRY. BUT OUTRAGE... YOUR OUTRAGE, NEEDED TO BE STOPPED.

IT WAS ALL I HAD LEFT...

IT WAS ALL I HAD LEFT OF *HIM!*

I COULD *BE* HIM, BE CLOSE TO HIM... ONLY AS LONG AS WE SHARED OUTRAGE.

ONLY FOR SO LONG AS I TOOK OUT MY REVENGE AND *HIS!*

YOU'VE TAKEN HIM AWAY FROM ME *AGAIN!*

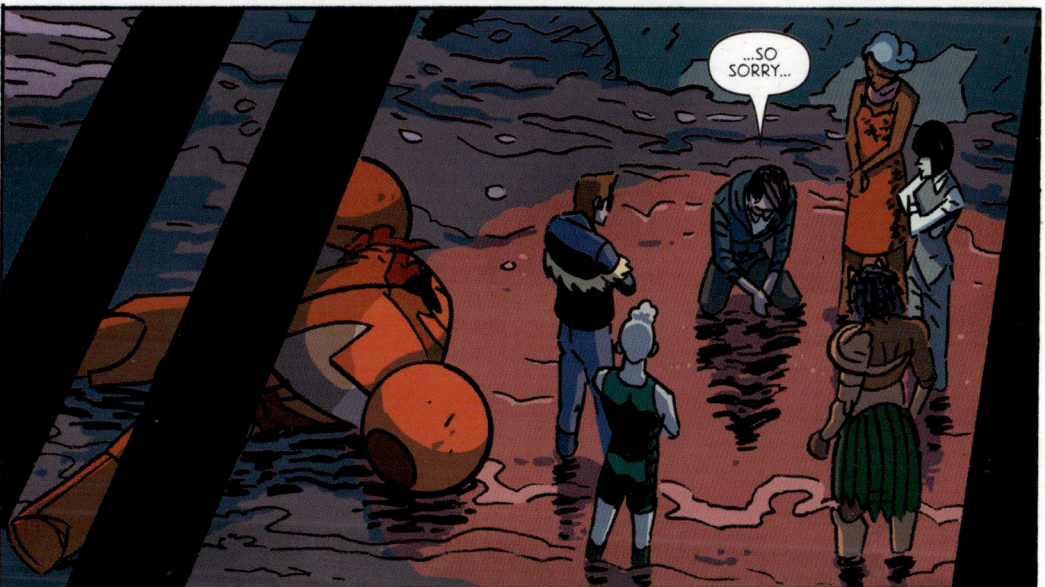

MOMENTS LATER...

GOOD JOB.

IS IT?

KID HAD TO BE STOPPED, WOLF.

I KNOW. BUT HE'S BEEN THROUGH *SO MUCH* ALREADY, I WISH WE DIDN'T HAVE TO GET SO... VIOLENT WITH THIS ONE.

AND HE'S NOT ENTIRELY WRONG. SOMETHING HAS TO BE DONE.

GAY BASHING AND HATE CRIME ARE STILL *FAR TOO* COMMON. WE ALL NEED TO BE DOING ALL WE CAN TO STOP IT.

WE KEEP KILLING AND KILLING, THEN THE KILLING JUST DON'T STOP, AND BEFORE LONG, WE'RE *ALL* BATHED IN BLOOD.

WE WILL BE. AS I'M SURE *YOU* WILL BE.

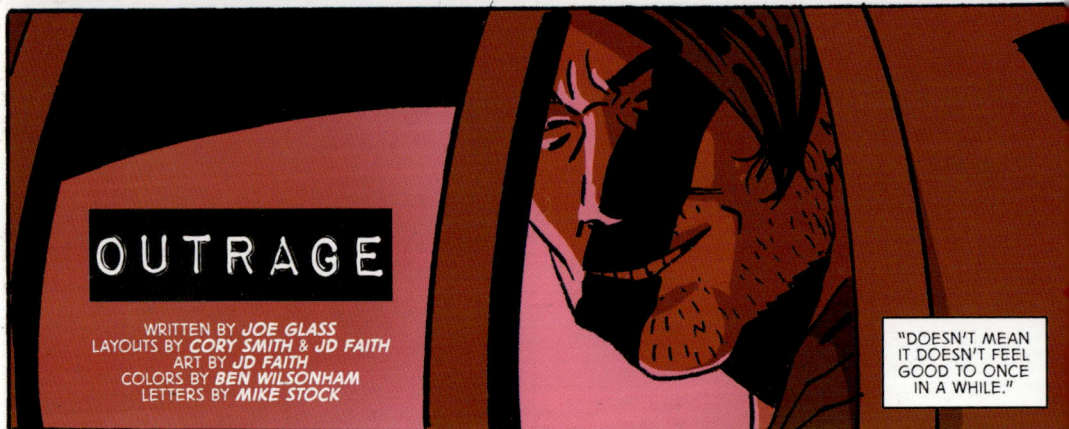

OUTRAGE

WRITTEN BY *JOE GLASS*
LAYOUTS BY *CORY SMITH* & *JD FAITH*
ART BY *JD FAITH*
COLORS BY *BEN WILSONHAM*
LETTERS BY *MIKE STOCK*

YOU CAN'T GO HOME AGAIN

END OF THE LINE, *POKER FACE!*

WRITER
JOE GLASS
ART
MARTIN KIRBY
COLOURS
BEN WILSONHAM
LETTERS
MIKE STOCK

OH, WOLFY.
WHERE YOU SEE AN END, I SEE A WAY OUT.
WHAT TH-?!
NO!
DAMMIT!
GOTCHA!
NICE CATCH, MUSCLES.
UMF
TELL ME: ARE YOU METAL INSIDE TOO?
WANT TO FIND OUT...
...OR IS THIS GETTING TOO HEAVY FOR YOU?
CRASH
LATER, SWEETHEART. GOOD GAME!

YOU OKAY?

SHE'S GETTING AWAY!

WE WON'T CATCH HER NOW. *TRUST ME,* SHE'LL SHOW AGAIN. SHE ALWAYS DOES.

WHAT'S HER DEAL ANYWAY? DID SHE FALL?

NOPE. JUMPED.

POKER FACE IS JUST AS HER NAME IMPLIES: UNPREDICTABLE, ALWAYS A MILLION STEPS AHEAD, AND *DAMN* LUCKY.

SOME PEOPLE THINK IT'S A POWER, BUT NO ONE'S EVER HELD ONTO HER LONG ENOUGH TO CHECK.

WHAT YOU DOIN' HERE ANYWAY, KID?

I WAS, UH, IN THE AREA.

UH HUH.

THEY CALLED AGAIN, HUH?

...

THERE REALLY IS NO KEEPING ANYTHING FROM YOU, IS THERE.

LATER

I MEAN, THEY SENT ME AWAY... TRIED TO *CURE* ME LIKE I WAS SICK. WHY WOULD THEY WANT ME BACK?

WHY WOULD *I* WANT *THEM?*

BECAUSE THEY'RE YOUR PARENTS, OWEN.

BUT I HAVEN'T CHANGED. I *WON'T.*

AND THAT DOESN'T MATTER. THEY'RE *STILL* YOUR PARENTS. YOU'RE *STILL* THEIR SON.

THAT'S SADLY MORE THAN A LOT OF PEOPLE GET. I NEVER GOT THE CHANCE TO SHARE EVERYTHING ABOUT MYSELF WITH MY PARENTS.

I'LL NEVER KNOW WHAT THEY'D HAVE THOUGHT OF THE MAN I BECAME.

AND SURE, *MAYBE* THEY HAVEN'T CHANGED EITHER, BUT IF YOU *DON'T* GO, YOU'LL ALWAYS WONDER.

AND THAT'S A BURDEN FEW CAN BARE. THEY'RE REACHING OUT TO YOU...

...MAYBE YOU SHOULD GIVE THEM A CHANCE.

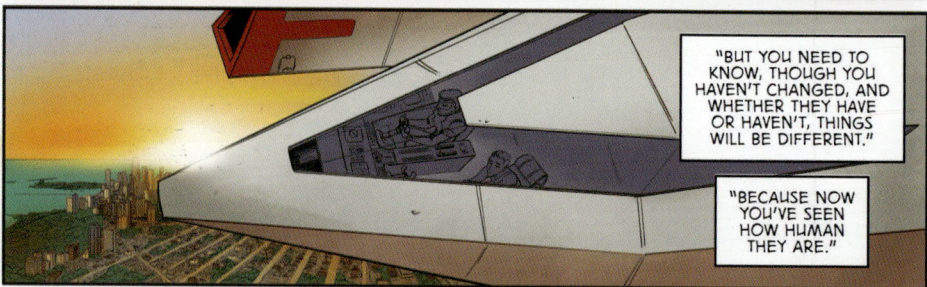

"BUT YOU NEED TO KNOW, THOUGH YOU HAVEN'T CHANGED, AND WHETHER THEY HAVE OR HAVEN'T, THINGS WILL BE DIFFERENT."

"BECAUSE NOW YOU'VE SEEN HOW HUMAN THEY ARE."

"THE WORLD IS *FULL* OF PEOPLE AFRAID OF WHAT'S DIFFERENT. AND SOMETIMES, WHEN IT COMES WITHIN THEIR HOMES, THEIR FAMILIES, THEY *LASH OUT.*"

"BUT THAT TRIAL GIVES 'EM THE OPPORTUNITY TO GROW. *TO LEARN.*"

"AND MOVE ON. BUT WE'LL ONLY MOVE ON IF WE TAKE THE RISK."

LATER

BYE, MOM. BYE, DAD.

WE'RE **SO** PROUD OF YOU, SWEETIE!

NOT STAYING?

NAH. YOU WERE RIGHT. THEY WERE JUST SCARED THAT MY POWERS WOULD GET ME IN DANGER. THEY FEEL TERRIBLE ABOUT WHAT THEY DID.

BUT THIS ISN'T MY HOME ANYMORE. MY PLACE IS WITH THE PRIDE.

THANKS FOR MAKING ME DO THIS.

NO PROBLEM, KID.

Y'KNOW, WOLF... I THINK YOUR PARENTS WOULD BE **REALLY PROUD** OF YOU TOO.

THANKS, KID.

"YOU THINK I SHOULD HAVE TOLD THEM ABOUT THE WHOLE FALLING OFF THE FIRE ESCAPE THING?"

"ONE STEP AT A TIME, KID."

218

OH COME ON, HARVEY, YOU *MUST* BE STARVING! AFTER ALL THAT 'EXERCISE' LAST NIGHT, HA!

UM, HARRY, ACTUALLY.

AND YEAH, KINDA, BUT I DON'T WANT TO IMPOSE OR ANYTHING.

NONSENSE!

JUST THINK OF IT AS A THANK YOU.

YOU'RE THE ONE WHO SAVED ME FROM MY HOUSE FIRE LAST NIGHT. AND THEN GAVE ME SOMEWHERE TO STAY.

AND YOU MORE THAN REPAID ME ALREADY FOR THAT.

MMM...

OH. MY. GOD! LOOKIT THE STATE OF ME!

OKAY, I *HAVE* TO JUMP IN THE SHOWER. MAKE YOURSELF AT HOME, HARRY, THE KITCHENS TOTALLY FULLY STOCKED!

THE MORNING AFTER

WRITTEN BY JOE GLASS   ART BY ADAM GRAPHITE   LETTERS BY MIKE STOCK

COME ON, I DON'T THINK WE'RE THE FIRST ONES UP FOR A CH--

OH, HI!

WHA-?!

UH, HI. I'M HARRY. I, UMM, I'M FABMAN'S... FRIEND.

UGH. MORNIN'.

YAWN

GULP

MORNING, CUB.

SORRY ABOUT THAT. HE'S A VERY... CONFIDENT GUY.

BUT HE HAD AN—

WELL, DUDE. IT IS THE MORNING...

BELIEVE IT OR NOT, HE'S STRAIGHT. BUT HE JUST DOESN'T SEEM TO MIND BEING... WELL, BARE AS THE DAY HE WAS BORN IN FRONT OF GAY DUDES.

SOMEONE SHOULD REALLY TALK TO THE KID ABOUT WEARING SOME CLOTHES IN COMPANY.

GOD-DAMMIT, CUB, PUT SOME CLOTHES ON!

222

MORNING.

NOW, DOES SOMEONE WANT TO TELL ME WHO THIS STRANGER IS AND WHY HE'S IN OUR HQ?

FABS BROUGHT HIM OVER, HE–

WHO ARE YOU? WHAT DO YOU WANT HERE?

I-I, UMM...

FABMAN SAVED ME WHEN MY APARTMENT CAUGHT FIRE AND I HAD NOWHERE TO STAY...

...AND HE OFFERED ME A BED HERE AND WELL, HE'S CUTE...

...AND I SAID SURE AND WELL WE JUST WOKE UP AND HE TOLD ME TO HAVE BREAKFAST...

...AND I'LL BE GONE SOON I SWEAR.

WOLF!

SIR!

COME NOW, WOLF. THIS IS NO WAY TO TREAT A GUEST!

FRIEND! YOU ARE WELCOME TO TAKE YOUR FILL OF WHATEVER WE HAVE TO OFFER. A WISE WARRIOR KNOWS THAT ONE MUST START ONES DAY BY BREAKING BREAD.

OH, DARLING, SOMETIMES YOU CAN BE SO DROLL. RELAX, YOUNG MAN.

SO TELL ME, YOUNG MAN. HOW IS THE PINK WONDER IN THE–

223

The Pride Adventures Issue 4 - Cover by Hamish Steele

CARDIFF, WALES, UK

CARDIFF MARDI GRAS, THE CITY'S ANNUAL LGBTQ EVENT.

GOOD EVENING, CARDIFF! AND WELCOME TO *MY* NIGHT!

DRAG EXTRAVAGANZA!!

AFTER ALL, YA CAN'T HAVE A DRAG EXTRAVAGANZA WITHOUT THE GREATEST DRAG QUEEN IN THE WORLD, *IMA SUPERSTAR!*

YOU *SUCK!*

OH, AND DID I FORGET TO MENTION, *HONEY?*

I ALSO HAVE *SUPERPOWERS!*

'CAUSE I'M THE MOST *FIERCE, SUPERPOWERED* DRAG QUEEN IN THE WORLD!

UH UH, HONEY...

226

OH, NO SHE BETTER DON'T

written by **JOE GLASS**   art by **GAVIN MITCHELL**   letters by **MIKE STOCK**

YOU AIN'T SNATCHING *THAT* TITLE!

ANGEL! AND YOUR NEW TEAM...

...HEARD YOU WEREN'T FIERCE ENOUGH TO HEAD OUT ALONE ANYMORE.

BUT YOU MUST BE DELUDED IF YA THINK YOU CAN BEAT *IMA SUPERSTAR!*

DON'T YOU JUST *LOVE* IT WHEN THEY START USING THE THIRD PERSON.

UH HUH, HONEY.

GUYS, LET'S STOP THIS FOOL.

C'MON, GUYS... LET'S DO THIS!

TRYING TO SCARE ME BY BEING ALL *BIG BAD?*

OH, HONEY...

THEY DON'T GET MUCH BIGGER THAN ME!

ANGEL, MY DATABASE SAYS IMA'S ABILITIES INCLUDE STEALING OTHER PEOPLE'S TALENTS...

...AND ARE *TIED* TO HER EGO...

...THE BIGGER *IT* GETS, THE MORE POWERFUL, AND BIGGER, *SHE* GETS.

OH, CHIL'... I GOT THIS.

HEY, DRAGZILLA! GET YOUR *FAT* BEHIND OVER HERE!

THE LIBRARY IS OPEN, HUNTY, AND YOU ARE *LOOOONG* OVERDUE!

GRRR!

MM-HMM, MISS THANG, TURN OVER HERE...

...NOT TOO FAST THOUGH, THAT WIG ALREADY LOOK LIKE IT GONNA DROP!

BUT HEY, HONEY, WITH THAT *MUG*, THAT *CHEAP WIG* IS THE LEAST O' YOUR WORRIES.

I MEAN, WHO TAUGHT YA T'PAINT, GURL? YOU LOOK LIKE YOU PAINTED A BEARD *ON*!

Wolf Files:
paint | verb
1 DRAG LINGO, to apply make up.

I'D TEACH YOU HOW TO BEAT THAT FACE, BUT HONEY, I AIN'T GOT ALL NIGHT.

Wolf Files:
beat | verb
1 DRAG LINGO, also to apply make up.

228

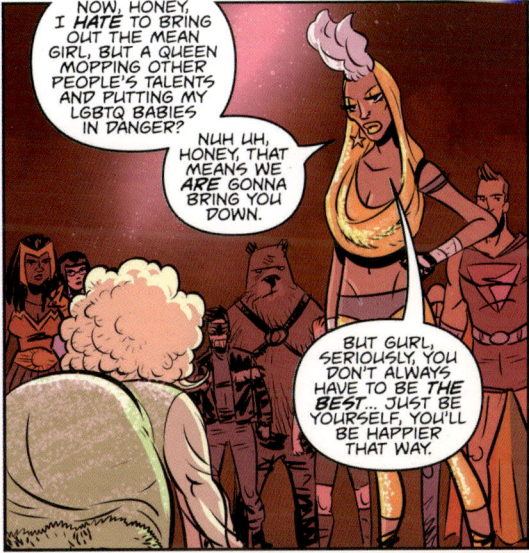

TIMES SQUARE, NEW YORK

YA WANT TO TAKE OUR GUNS! IT'S OUR *CONSTITUTIONAL RIGHT*! YOU WON'T TAKE *MY RIGHTS* FROM ME!

OY... REALLY?

READY, TWINK?

OH, YOU HAVE *NO* IDEA... BOMBS AWAY, FABS!

TNK

GUN MACHINE

WRITTEN BY JOE GLASS ~ ART BY ANDY CLIFT
COLORS BY BEN WILSONHAM ~ LETTERS BY MIKE STOCK

OPEN UP

WRITTEN BY
JOE GLASS

ART BY
TANA FORD

COLORS BY
BEN WILSONHAM

LETTERS BY
MIKE STOCK

OH, HELL NO!

WHAT THE-?

COME NOW, DEARY.

NONE OF THOSE ARE REALLY YOUR STYLE AT ALL.

SHOULD I BE TEACHING YOU FASHION SENSE, OR JUST THE BASIC MORALS OF STEALING?

HERE IS A HINT, SCOUNDREL.

IT IS NOT GOOD.

GERR- OFF ME!

237

"IF YOU... *PRIDE* YOURSELF ON DRINKING GREAT MILKSHAKES... UGH... THEN YOU NEED TO HEAD *STRAIGHT* DOWN TO THE YARD FOR OUR TWO-FOR-ONE SUMMER SPECIAL..."

THE ★YARD

WRITTEN BY MIKE GARLEY - ART BY CHRIS IMBER
COLORS BY BEN WILSONHAM - LETTERS BY MIKE STOCK

YOU *REALLY* WANT ME TO READ THIS?

WE 'DONATED' A *LOT* OF MONEY TO CHARITY SO YOU WOULD.

LISTEN KID, AFTER WHAT'S HAPPENED - YOU'RE IN, YOUR TEAM'S IN, THE WHOLE LGBBQ WAVE IS IN!

AND MILKSHAKES AS GREAT AS OURS ARE *ALWAYS* IN!

SO JUST ENJOY YOUR MILKSHAKE, SAY YOUR LINES, SMILE FOR THE CAMERA, AND ENJOY YOUR FIVE MINUTES OF FAME, YEAH?

WHAT DO YOU MEAN 'FIVE MINUTES OF FAME'?

OH, YOU KNOW! THESE FLAVOUR OF THE MONTH CAUSES. THEY'RE BIG MONEY.

AND BY YOU HAVING YOU HERE IT HELPS US *ALL.*

MORE PRIME TIME TV MEANS WE HELP NORMALIZE YOUR STUFF, AND BY US HAVING *YOU* HERE IT SHOWS THAT WE'RE 'WITH YOU'.

OBVIOUSLY NOT WITH-YOU, WITH-YOU.

THAT'S WHY WE ASKED SPECIFICALLY FOR *YOU*. THE STRAIGHT ONE.

US STRAIGHT WHITE GUYS NEED TO STICK TOGETHER, YOU KNOW?

SLURRPPPRRPP

239

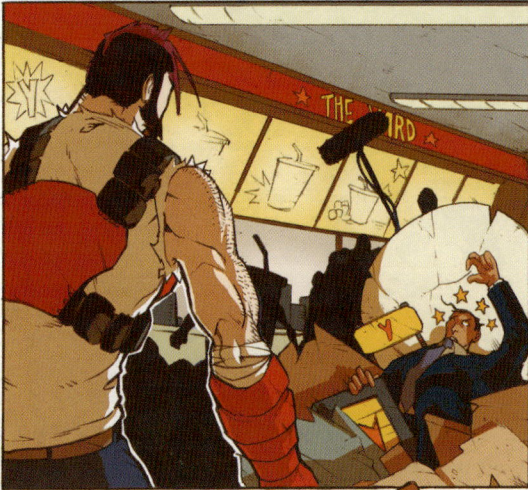

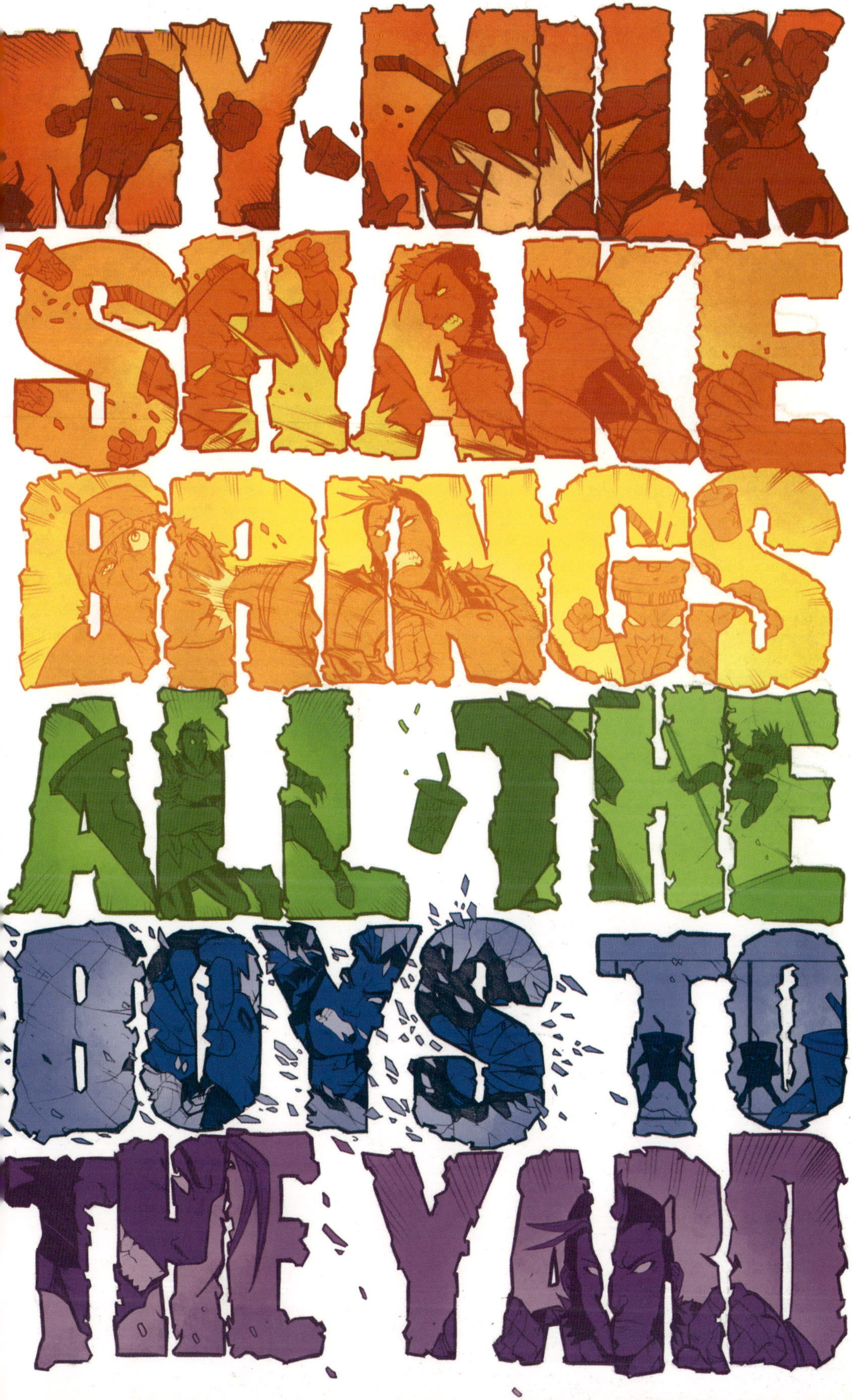
MY MILK
SHAKE
BRINGS
ALL THE
BOYS TO
THE YARD

COME TOGETHER

written by
JOE GLASS
art by
ANDY BENNETT
letters by
MIKE STOCK

246

THE PACK

A PRIDE STORY

WRITTEN BY
JOE GLASS

ART BY
BEN WILSONHAM

LETTERS BY
MIKE STOCK

THE RED TIGERS HAVE BEEN MAKING MEETINGS LIKE THIS ALL OVER CHICAGO.

THIS IS THE FIRST TIME I'VE BEEN HERE IN TIME TO CATCH THE DEALER.

ME AGAINST THESE FIVE...

...THIS SHOULD BE FUN.

TAKING OUT THE ARMED IDIOTS FIRST SHOULD BE EASY.

FAST AND HARD. JUST TAKE 'EM DOWN.

DAMN! SHOOT 'IM ALREADY!

YOU THINK I AIN'T TRYIN'?!

A COUPLE TASER-DISCS TAKE DOWN THE OTHER TWO.

DEALER IS NEXT.

THE KEY IS TO FIGHT SMART.

SMALL, CRITICAL STRIKES.

TAKING DOWN THE TARGET WITH A THOUSAND CUTS.

TAKE OUT THE HAMSTRING. IMMOBILISE THE TARGET.

OR NOT.

TECHNOLOGICAL AUGMENTATION IS FAIRLY COMMON.

IN A WORLD WHERE PEOPLE GET SUPERPOWERS, THOSE THAT DON'T OFTEN TRY TO FIND WAYS TO LEVEL THE PLAYING FIELD.

NOT EVERYONE CAN AFFORD THE KINDS OF BIOLOGICAL AND GENETIC AUGMENTATION THAT FROST HAS.

NOT SEEN THIS LEVEL OF AUGMENTATION IN... EVER.

THE PRIDE

ORIGINS

RUNNING ORDER

WOLF

Written by Joe Glass, Art by Marc Ellerby

WHITE TRASH

Written by Joe Glass, Art by Joshua Faith

ANGEL

Story and Art by Joe Glass, Colors by Kris Carter, Letters by Mike Stock

MUSCLE MARY

Written by Joe Glass, Art by Cory Smith, Colors by Kris Carter, Letters by Mike Stock

BEAR

Written by Joe Glass, Art by Ryan Cody, Letters by Mike Stock

FABMAN

Written by Joe Glass, Art by Jack Lawrence, Letters by Mike Stock

FROST

Written by Joe Glass, Art by Héctor Barros, Letters by Mike Stock

TWINK

Written by Joe Glass, Art by Jacopo Camagni, Letters by Mike Stock

WOLF

WORDS: JOSEPH GLASS
ART: MARC ELLERBY

SO, LIKE, YOU GUYS THINK THIS... *WOLF* DUDE SHOULD BE IN *THE JUSTICE DIVISION?*

IN HIS CIVILIAN IDENTITY, WHICH IS PUBLICLY UNKNOWN, WOLF IS *BRIAN WILDE*, HEAD OF THE MASSIVE ENERGY, ENVIRONMENTAL AND PROPRIETARY TECHNOLOGY CONCERN *WILDE CORPORATION*.

INHERITED WHEN HIS PARENTS DIED IN A *CAR CRASH* WHEN HE WAS JUST *17* YEARS OF AGE, HE'D ALREADY SPENT MANY YEARS TRAINING HIS BODY AND MIND FOR WHAT HE SAW AS HIS PERSONAL MISSION.

HE HAS NO POWERS, INSTEAD WORKING HARD TO REACH PEAK PHYSICAL FITNESS. HE HAS TRAINED IN NUMEROUS MARTIAL ARTS. WITH HIS RESOURCES, HE CREATES ANY EQUIPMENT HE NEEDS.

HE'S TRAINED HIS MIND TOO, GRADUATING WITH DEGREES IN CRIMINOLOGY, CHEMISTRY AND BUSINESS.

KRAKOW

IN HIS HOME OF CHICAGO, HE'S ACHIEVED HIS *GREATEST* SUCCESS.

Chicago Tribune

WOLF WINS

Crime Fighter Takeson mob and wins

PROVING A MASTER INVESTIGATOR TOO, HE TOOK DOWN EVERY SINGLE CRIME BOSS IN ONE FELL SWOOP, PROVIDING ENOUGH EVIDENCE TO PUT THEM ALL AWAY FOR GOOD.

COOL.

OKAY, DUDE. I GET IT. THIS GUY'S PRETTY GOOD, HUH.

'KAY, I GUESS HE'S IN.

COOL.

WOLF
a.k.a. Brian Wilde

Powers:
Peak physical fitness.
Martial arts.
Keen scientific mind
and detective!

WHITE TRASH

WRITTEN BY JOE GLASS
ART AND LETTERS BY JOSHUA FAITH

GOOD EVENING AMERICA! THIS IS TRISHA MORGAN WITH YOUR WEEKLY CAPES.TV 'IN THE SPOTLIGHT' REPORT!

CAPES SPOTLIGHT!

THIS WEEKS FEATURED HERO IS LA STREET LEVEL AVENGER, *WHITE TRASH!*

WHITE TRASH GREW UP IN SOUTH CENTRAL LA, AND IT WAS A HARD PLACE TO BE.

MY DAD WAS A DRUNK, SIMPLE AS THAT. WE LIVED IN A HOLE, SURROUNDED BY OTHER DRUNKS, DEALERS, EVERYTHING.

IT WASN'T EXACTLY THE PERFECT PLACE TO RAISE A KID. AND I KNEW I WAS... DIFFERENT.

TROUBLE IS, DAD KNEW IT TOO.

WOW. IT'S AMAZING YOU DIDN'T TURN OUT TO BE A VILLAIN.

TOO MUCH OF THAT IN THE WORLD ALREADY. I WANTED TO BE SOMETHING DIFFERENT.

I SAW THE WORLD AROUND ME AND WANTED TO MAKE IT BETTER.

I DREW STRENGTH FROM THAT CONVICTION. STRENGTH I TOOK HOME.

AND ONE DAY, WHEN POP WAS THAT LITTLE BIT TOO DRUNK AND CRAZY...

...AND I JUST THOUGHT 'ENOUGH IS ENOUGH'.

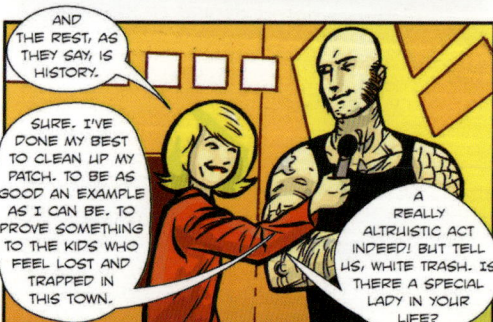

AND THE REST, AS THEY SAY, IS HISTORY.

SURE. I'VE DONE MY BEST TO CLEAN UP MY PATCH. TO BE AS GOOD AN EXAMPLE AS I CAN BE. TO PROVE SOMETHING TO THE KIDS WHO FEEL LOST AND TRAPPED IN THIS TOWN.

A REALLY ALTRUISTIC ACT INDEED! BUT TELL US, WHITE TRASH. IS THERE A SPECIAL LADY IN YOUR LIFE?

NO. COMMENT.

WHITE TRASH

A.K.A. WAYNE MATHERS

POWERS: SUPER-STRENGTH AND INVULNERABILITY DIRECTLY CORRELATED TO HIS CONFIDENCE AND STRENGTH OF CONVICTION.

Story by
JOE GLASS

Art by
CORY SMITH

Colours by
KRIS CARTER

Letters by
MIKE STOCK

MUSCLE MARY

BEHOLD! THE HIDDEN ISLAND OF LABRYSIA, HOME OF THE SAPPHONS! SECRET NATION OF MIGHTY WOMYN, POWER, COMPASSION AND SISTERHOOD THEIR GOALS.

LO! HERE SITS HER WONDROUSNESS, QUEEN GRACE OF THE SAPPHONS! AND EVER AT HER SIDE, HER MIGHTY AND CARING DAUGHTER, PRINCESS SAPPHIRE.

MANY THOUSANDS OF YEAS THIS JEWEL OF CIVILISATION HAS REMAINED UNDISTURBED BY MAN. THOUSANDS OF YEARS, RUINED IN ONE DAY.

HER BEAUTY AND STRENGTH, QUEEN GRACE BESTOWS THE HONOUR OF HER PRESENCE TO THE MEN.

YOUR MAJESTY...

SOME ACCEPT GRACIOUSLY—

SOME SEE ONLY AN OPPORTUNITY.

BLAM

NO!

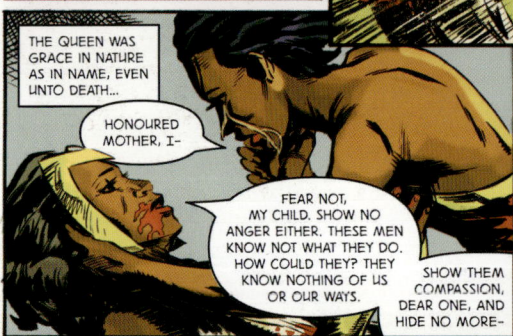

THE QUEEN WAS GRACE IN NATURE AS IN NAME, EVEN UNTO DEATH...

HONOURED MOTHER, I—

FEAR NOT, MY CHILD. SHOW NO ANGER EITHER. THESE MEN KNOW NOT WHAT THEY DO. HOW COULD THEY? THEY KNOW NOTHING OF US OR OUR WAYS.

SHOW THEM COMPASSION, DEAR ONE, AND HIDE NO MORE—

I SHALL GO UNTO THE WORLD OF MAN, AND LOOK FOR THE GOOD THAT I HOPE DWELLS THERE.

AND IF I FIND IT WANTING, THEN SHALL WE SEE FIT TO CORRECT THEM.

AND WITH THE LABRYX OF METIS, I SHALL HAVE THE STRENGTH TO SPREAD OUR MESSAGE.

MEDEA, THE EVER-ANGRY, HEAD OF THE QUEEN'S GUARD...

THESE MEN MUST DIE FOR THIS TRANS-GRESSION!

NO!

THEY WILL BE SHOWN COMPASSION HERE, THAT THEY MAY KNOW ITS TASTE.

SO SAY I, YOUR... ...YOUR QUEEN.

CS

THIRTY YEARS BY THE TELLING OF MAN HAS SHE LIVED AMONG US. DUBBED 'MUSCLE MARY' BY THE REVELLERS OF A FESTIVAL MOST GAY WHEN SHE ARRIVED, SHE HAS FOUND GOOD AND BAD, AND DONE ONLY GOOD IN RETURN. HER MISSION CONTINUES...

SAPPHIRE
POWERS: IMMENSE STRENGTH, DURABILITY, SPEED, FLIGHT. LONG LIVED, SKILLED WARRIOR.

THE BEAR

Written by Joe Glass
Illustrated by Ryan Cody
Lettered by Mike Stock

I WEREN'T ALWAYS THE MAN-BEAR I AM TODAY.

WELL, I GUESS I WAS ALWAYS A 'BEAR', HUH, JUST NOT *THE* BEAR!

AN' MOREOVER, I WEREN'T ALWAYS GAY EITHER. OR I WAS, BUT I WASN'T... COMFORTABLE WITH IT.

I WAS RAISED TO BELIEVE IN FAMILY, A GOOD, HARD DAYS WORK. AND I... I MARRIED SARAH, THINKING THAT MY HEART WOULD GET INTO THAT SOMEDAY TOO.

LIKE I SAID, I WAS UNCOMFORTABLE IN MY OWN SKIN. MY HEART KNEW IT...

...MY BODY WOULD SOON TOO.

WHAT I THOUGHT WAS A BAD CASE A' FLU TURNED OUT TO BE SO MUCH MORE.

I WAS X-CEL VIRUS POSITIVE, I WAS JUST A LATE BLOOMER...IN MORE'N ONE CASE.

SARAH CERTAINLY DIDN'T TAKE TO THE NEW LOOK, CAN'T BLAME 'ER. BUT SHE REALLY HATED THE MAGAZINES...

SHE LEFT ME AFTER THAT. CAN'T BLAME 'ER. WOULDN'T HEAR FROM HER AGAIN IN YEARS, BUT THEN, I WASN'T THINKING MUCH ABOUT THAT THEN.

I FINALLY CAME TO TERMS WITH WHO I WAS, BUT IT WAS SO LATE... I HAD NO IDEA WHAT I WAS DOING.

I WASN'T REALLY THINKING AT THIS TIME. I DID THINGS. THINGS I AIN'T PROUD OF.

AND I MADE MISTAKES.

I'M... I'M SORRY, BABY. BUT I THINK... I THINK I'M GAY.

MISTAKES THAT'LL AFFECT THE REST OF MY LIFE.

BUT HEY, WE ALL MAKE MISTAKES.

IT'S HOW WE LIVE WITH 'EM; WHAT WE DO AFTERWARDS THAT COUNTS.

FOR ME, I EDUCATE KIDS ON THE SCENE SO THEY DON'T MAKE THE SAME MISTAKES I DO.

AND HEY, I'M STRONG, SO I DO MY PART TO PROTECT MY COMMUNITY TOO, ANY WAY I CAN.

AND LUCKILY I FOUND GOOD FRIENDS ALONG THE WAY TO HELP ME OUT.

THE BEAR AKA

HARVEY CASTRO

POWERS:
animal keen senses, enhanced strength and agility. Bear-like appearance.

SO THA'S ME. I FIGHT FOR WHAT'S RIGHT, NO MATTER WHAT.

'CAUSE WE ALL MAKE MISTAKES, BUT WE DON'T HAVE TO BE DEFINED BY 'EM.

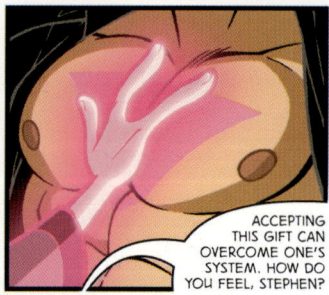

FROST

THANKS FOR TAKING THE TIME, MS...?

FROST, DEAR.

RIGHT. SO, WE ALREADY KNOW YOU WERE BORN INTO AN ARISTOCRATIC FAMILY IN THE UK. YOU NEVER WANTED FOR ANYTHING.

WELL, EXCEPT FOR POWERS IT SEEMS. WE KNOW YOURS AREN'T NATURAL.

YOU HAD EXTENSIVE SURGERY TO ENHANCE CERTAIN... ATTRIBUTES, AND GIVE YOU YOUR ICE MANIPULATION POWERS.

WELL, YOU'VE DONE VERY WELL BY YOURSELF SO FAR, DEARIE.

WE JUST NEED YOU TO FILL IN THE GAPS.

MY EDITOR WANTS A COMPREHENSIVE STORY.

LIKE, WE KNOW THAT AFTER YOUR SURGERIES, YOUR FAMILY DISOWNED YOU.

BUT WE DON'T KNOW WHY.

YOU'RE FAMILY NAME WAS RYDER, RIGHT? YOU HAD A BROTHER BY THE NAME OF... EDWARD?

VERY GOOD. VERY GOOD INDEED.

TELL ME, YOU'RE STORY. IT'S ALL ON THERE?

UMM, YEAH, I...

HEY! WHAT THE HELL?!

I PAID A LOT OF MONEY TO MAKE MYSELF WHAT I AM TODAY.

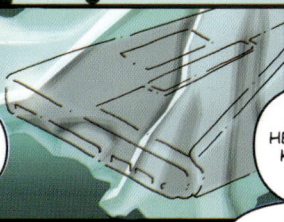

THE ICE-COLD HEADMISTRESS KEEPING THE MASSES IN LINE.

I PAID EVEN MORE TO MAKE MY PAST DISAPPEAR.

IT WOULDN'T COST MUCH MORE TO MAKE SURE IT STAYS THAT WAY.

REMEMBER THAT, WON'T YOU, DARLING?

WRITTEN BY JOE GLASS

ART BY HECTOR BARROS

LETTERS BY MIKE STOCK

FROST

A.K.A. EVANGELINE ISOBELLA RYDER III
POWERS: ICE AND TEMPERATURE MANIPULATION.

TWINK

WRITTEN BY *JOE GLASS*
ART BY *JACOPO CAMAGNI*
LETTERS BY *MIKE STOCK*

DEAR MOM AND DAD,

I SUPPOSE YOU SHOULD KNOW THAT I'M OKAY...IF YOU REALLY CARE. I'M WRITING THIS LETTER TO TRY AND FIGURE THAT OUT MYSELF.

IT'S NOT LIKE IT WAS A SURPRISE I WANTED TO BE A SUPERHERO. IT'S ALL I EVER WANTED TO BE.

I ACTUALLY TRAINED FOR IT THOUGH. I WAS GOING TO BE THE BEST. WHETHER I HAD POWERS OR NOT.

I WON AT SPORTS, I WORKED HARD. BUT ALL YOU GUYS EVER SAW WAS HOW 'DANGEROUSLY' DIFFERENT I WAS BECOMING.

THEN ONE DAY...

GET OUTTA TH' WAY!

OH MY GOD!

...THE X-CEL VIRUS FINALLY REACTED WITH MY GENES AND I FINALLY GOT ALL I WANTED.

I'D NEVER BEEN HAPPIER.

YEEE EEAA AAAH!

BUT NOT YOU GUYS.

INSTEAD, YOU SEND ME TO A PRISON CAMP, RUN BY A MAD MAN WHO CLAIMED HE COULD 'CURE' ME.

AND YOU LEFT ME.

WELL, I GOT OUT OF THAT PLACE. I WON'T TELL YOU WHERE I AM.

AND I'M GONNA FIND PEOPLE JUST LIKE ME AND BE HAPPY AGAIN.

...JUST ...HAPPY AGAIN. MA... ...'LL SEE ME ON ...EWS.

LOVE, FRO... OWEN

TWINK

A.K.A.
OWEN MERCURY

POWERS:
ORGANIC METAL BODY.
STRONGER THAN STEEL,
MORE LUSTROUS THAN
PLATINUM.

BEHIND THE SCENES

GAVIN MITCHELL

Wolf was a fairly difficult character to come up with a design for, and I really just had a vague idea on the kind of hero that Wolf was, and some random ideas for look. We wound up with a ton of designs, but finally settled on the fantastic design from Gavin that people have really responded to.

My one suggestion for Gav on WT was to look at the model/artist/actor Trevor Wayne… which of course meant lots of tattoos. I'm sure all the artists on the series loved me for that.

Originally, Frost was a blonde and wore all white, but we felt that this made her look too similar to a character belonging to a certain House of Ideas.

We had a few design ideas to redesign the character, and sort of ultimately went with a kind of Marlene Dietrich vibe.

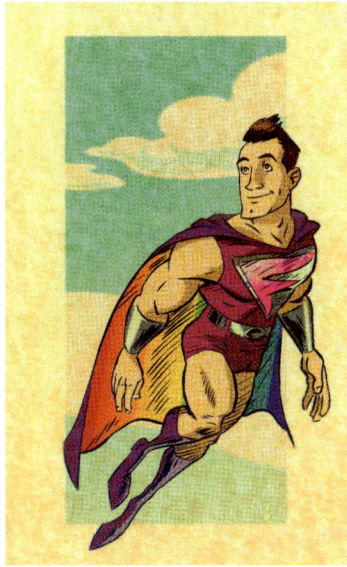

KRIS ANKA

Kris redesigned Outrage for his second appearance onward, to suggest Jai Wing continuing to upgrade his tech. As you can see, he included a reference for where the wearer is in the suit. It was Kris who came up with the floating gauntlets/hands idea, and I admit, initially I was reticent. But then the action sequence possibilities started flooding into my mind, and it just cemented my assertion that Kris is a creative genius!

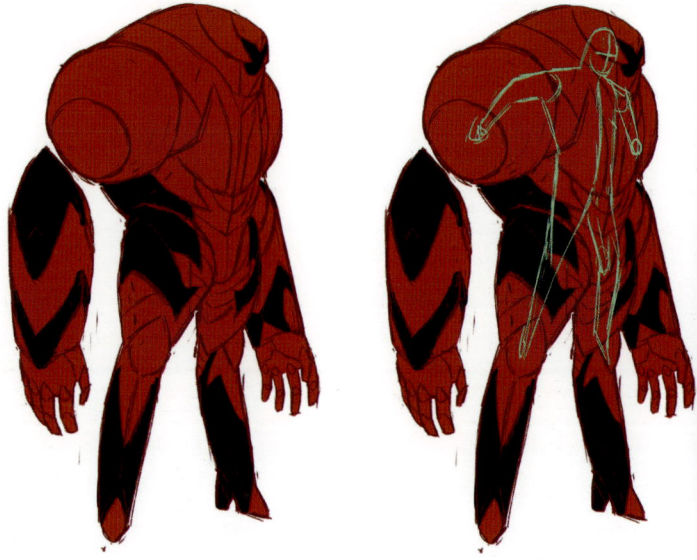

Kris started working on these awesome bust sketches for the whole team (below), which are just incredible.

Kris's design for the King Lion villain who appeared in The Pride Adventures #2 (right).

Some unused cover design ideas (below).

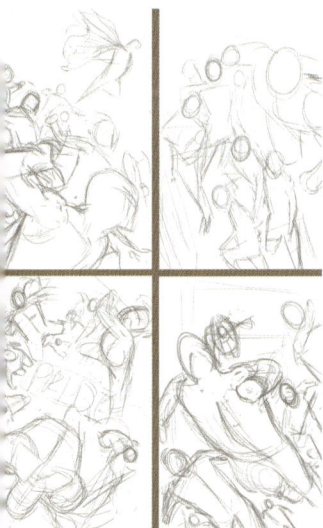

Sophie found the time to help design the last member of The Pride, who was joining in a late issue, and came up with this final design for Bear's son, Cub

orbes came on to do the cover
or The Pride Adventures #2,
ut also helped to design villain
oker Face who would appear
n the next issue.

le created this fantastic design
nd inspiration sheet for the
haracter.

bomberstyle
jacket

Maxime's designs for The Pride's jet, the Cruiser (left).

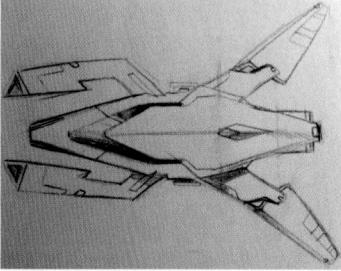

Maxime had to create detailed character notes and design sheets, that really added new levels of detail and distinction to the characters.

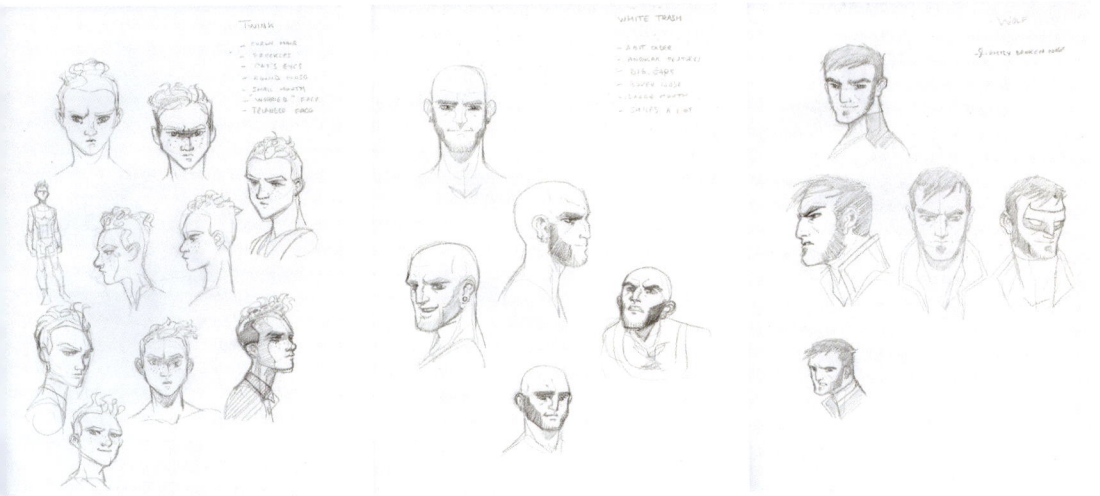

HECTOR BARROS

Maxime, with fellow artist Hector Barros, had also started working on these individual character shots to get a feel for the team. They finished Frost, FabMan and Angel, and here's also the linework for a Bear piece.

JOE GLASS

For a few of the characters,
I made some sketches myself.
You can probably see why
I don't tend to draw very often.

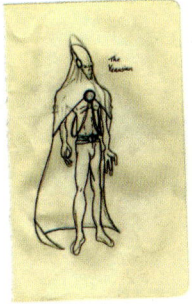

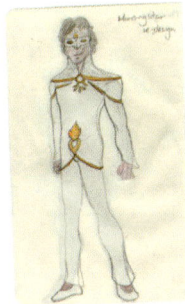

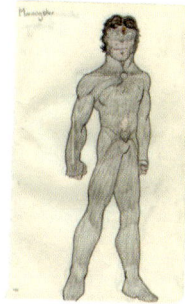

MARTIN KIRBY

Martin came on to actually
draw the story containing
Poker Face, and expanded and
streamlined the original design
for the character.

Here's some variations on his
final design.

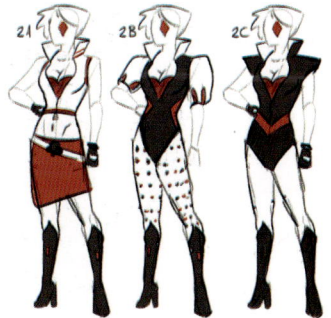

CHRISTIAN WILDGOOSE

THE PRIDE
BEAR

THE PRIDE
CUB

THE PRIDE ADVENTURES · THE LIONESSES

Chris did some much needed character design sheets to get a feel for some of the characters appearing in his pages (this page and overleaf).

Chris did the design for the Lionesses, the back-up/lieutenants in King Lion's gang (bottom left).

Because Christian is an incredible talent, he just had to create a working plan for the training room too (overleaf)!

CHRISTIAN WILDGOOSE

THE PRIDE
TWINK

THE PRIDE
WOLF

THE PRIDE
TRAINING ROOM

TRAINING DROID

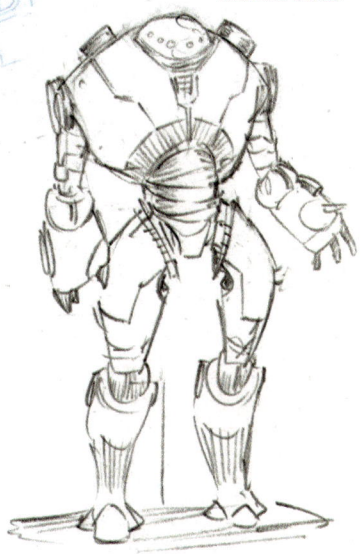

TRAINING ROOM FLOOR - OVERHEAD

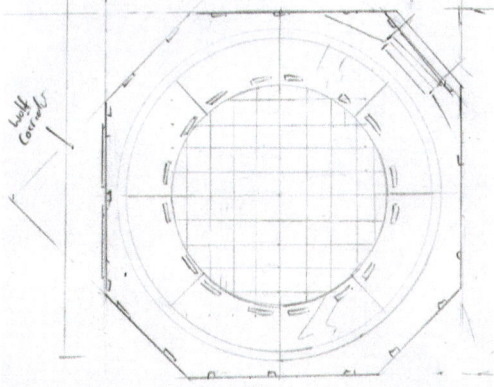

main door

AFTERWORD

Well, that's it, everyone.

All of *The Pride*, and more, in one place. And we couldn't have done it without you.

I want to say a massive thank you again to everyone who has funded through the Kickstarter, but also to all those who have been supporting *The Pride* from day one.

The book has been coming out now for seven years. A lengthy, and at times difficult and frustrating production, every bit of which has been a lesson and welcome challenge. The support from all of the readers, and those who have come and talked to me at cons about the themes and story of the project, has made every second of the journey absolutely worthwhile. That my little idea can be something that others enjoy and want to see in the world... there's no more gratifying and wonderful feeling than I have ever come across.

Because really *The Pride* has been going on even older. I was tinkering away with characters and scenes from way back when; those seemingly ancient days when I was a comic reading teenager coming to terms with his sexuality. All I ever wanted to see was a character that was just like me, not an allegory, not a whispered fact never appearing in the actual stories, but an open, honest and true representation. After years of uncertainty and tinkering, finally I put the idea out into the world, even if it was only for me.

Thankfully, I guess there are others out there who wanted the same thing.

Comics, as a medium, have come along a long way since we begun. Diversity and representation improves and declines in a semi-regular peak and trough, but the peaks seem to be getting higher, the troughs shallower, and when we do hit low points, the public outcry seems to be louder than ever. There's still a long way to go.

The Pride, therefore, will keep on going. I hope you decide to stay on the ride.

Joe Glass

THANK YOU FOR READING AND SUPPORTING THE PRIDE!

MERCI

DANKE

KIITOS

DIOLCH

TACK!

THE PRIDE WILL RETURN...

ART BY LUCIANO VECCHIO